Just for the Record

CHARLES AMER
with John Wilson

*To Shaun
Best Wishes
Charles Amer*

PARKWAY

First published in Great Britain by
PARKWAY
Marton Hotel and Country Club
Stokesley Road, Marton,
Middlesbrough, TS7 8DS
1998

Copyright Charles Amer 1998

Photographs supplied by the Charles Amer archive.

The right of Charles Amer to be identified as the author of this book has been asserted in accordance with the Copyright, Designs and Patents Act 1988.

All rights reserved. No part of this publication may be reproduced, stored in a retrieval system, or transmitted in any form or by means, electronic, mechanical, photocopying, recording or otherwise without the prior permission in writing of the copyright holder, nor be circulated in any form or binding or cover other than in which it is published.

ISBN 0 9 532 1310 2

Typesetting and Origination by:
P's & Q's Ltd., Unit 10, Gibraltar Row,
King Edward Industrial Estate, Liverpool L3 7HJ.

Printed and bound by:
Albion Graphics, Old Connolly Complex,
Kirkby Bank Road, Knowsley Industrial Park,
Kirkby, Merseyside, L33 7SY.

Acknowledgements

I wish to acknowledge the major contribution made by John Wilson in the production of this book. Without his powers of persuasion, endless patience and unstinting assistance, its publication would not have been possible.

JOHN WILSON is a graduate of the Open University, a former deputy headteacher and college education lecturer. He was co-author of the highly acclaimed and award winning book on Middlesbrough Football Club called "Ayresome Park Memories" and firmly believes that without knowledge of the past, you cannot understand the future.

Dedication

To all my Loyal Staff and Patrons.

CONTENTS

Preface		9
1	A Remarkable Recovery	10
2	Hi De Hi	26
3	Strike Up The Band	50
4	And The Band Played On	62
5	Variety Is The Spice Of Life	76
6	Renovation And Construction	87
7	Right Place Right Time	103
8	Hotels And Roundabouts	121
9	Ayresome Fully Aired	132
10	Resignation	166
11	The So Called Great White Elephant	173
12	Years In Limbo	190
13	Inspiration And Recognition	198

PREFACE

THERE comes a time in everyone's life when you have to say enough is enough. I have now reached that point. Recent authorised publications purporting to examine the true story about certain events with which I was connected at Middlesbrough Football Club over 15 years ago, have once again only succeeded in adding to the already considerable existing volume of unsubstantiated, misinformation and innuendo duping the people of Teesside.

After winning a High Court libel action against the Private Eye magazine in the 1980s it was always my intention to retain a dignified silence with regard to the circumstances surrounding that litigation process, despite the years of misery it caused my family and the irreparable damage it did to my personal reputation.

Even after all this time, however, it appears there are still certain individuals who are determined to laboriously rake over old ground in a patently obvious attempt to permanently tarnish the Amer name. This is a situation which I cannot allow to continue any longer.

So, after much consideration and consultation, I have come to the conclusion that not only should the facts with regard to my involvement with Middlesbrough Football Club be made public, but I should also utilise this opportunity to share and expand on some of the detailed personal background information I painstakingly prepared for the aforementioned court case.

It was only as a result of formally recording and reviewing my experiences for the benefit of my defence counsel, Geoffrey Shaw QC, that I became aware, and indeed was genuinely surprised, by how varied and rewarding a life it has been.

The following reminiscences, I hope, will be particularly appreciated by those people who through the years holidayed with me at Butlin's, danced to my big band, visited my hotels and supported Middlesbrough FC while I was a director and chairman of the board.

There are always two sides to every story and it's about time people read mine.

CHARLES AMER 1998

CHAPTER ONE

A Remarkable Recovery

I've no recollection of any involvement in a road traffic accident. My memory of the crash, in the autumn of 1929, is a total blank. Apparently it was so horrific that the impact hurled me into the air like a large rag doll and, as I landed, I became impaled on the spiked iron railings of Dorman Long's Club in South Bank.

I sustained multiple injuries which included a fractured skull, a partly dismembered right arm and a broken right leg with deep lacerations. The trauma was so severe and life threatening that even the local press prematurely reported the death of an 18-year-old youth whose motorbike had been in collision with a car at Branch End on the road to Middlesbrough.

I have to confess in all honesty, it was an accident waiting to happen because I treated the streets of Middlesbrough as my own private racetrack. I simply loved the thrill of riding my Norton 350cc at breakneck speed. There was no compulsory use of crash helmets in those days, so with the throttle wide open and the wind lashing into my face, motorbike riding was a truly exhilarating experience.

The timing of the accident was unfortunate however, because I'd just begun to race competitively at events organised by two of the well known local riders of that time, Freddie Dixon and Ronnie Parkinson, on Redcar sands and Hartlepool promenade.

In fact I was planning to take race riding more seriously in the future. I was mechanically proficient and could strip down and rebuild an engine. I also received positive encouragement to participate from my father, Charles, and he often helped me with the bike's fine tuning.

Seventy years ago sand racing was a fully recognised sport with a prominent British Championship and a national list of fixtures. The events attracted huge crowds, particularly at Redcar, where the long promenade provided the public with the perfect spectator vantage point.

Anyone could enter the heats regardless of their ability and with top prizes of around five guineas for the victor there was no shortage of entrants. Although I never troubled the judges I did thoroughly enjoy taking part, except for one event at Hartlepool where I lost control of the bike and crashed into the sea wall. Luckily I escaped unscathed with only my pride dented.

Major traffic accidents do however intermittently punctuate my life. One freezing winter's night in January, during the Second World War, I was travelling back from a dance at the Crown Hotel in Whitby when my S.S. sports car skidded on Skelton Bank, went straight through the S-bend, ploughed into a telegraph pole, rolled over repeatedly and ended upside down in an ice-cold stream.

If that occurance wasn't shocking enough, as I was being slowly extracated from the smouldering wreckage by a kind hearted cyclist who was quickly on the scene, the car suddenly blew up, showering red hot metal in all directions. I was extremely fortunate only to be detained overnight in Guisborough Hospital with severe concussion.

I survived to tell the tale thanks to the timely intervention of the cyclist, to whom I gave a watch to convey my appreciation for his unselfish bravery. If it hadn't been for his prompt action I may well have died in the ensuing inferno.

Another motoring incident occurred in the 1930's when I owned a large Standard Nine which was a real tank of a car. I was travelling on the main trunk road through Brambles Farm in Middlesbrough when I was hit by a car which emerged without warning from a side road. The severity of the impact turned my vehicle over twice. Luckily I again escaped without a scratch, which was a sound endorsement of how solidly my vehicle was constructed, bearing in mind that over 40 years ago there were no restraining seat belts fitted.

After my motorbike accident in South Bank I was unconscious for about ten weeks. During the whole time my mother Kate, with whom I always had a very caring relationship, kept a constant vigil at my bedside. My stay in North Ormesby General Hospital eventually lasted for over eight months.

At one stage my mother was told my right arm was so badly mutilated the doctors were even contemplating amputation to at least enhance my slim chances of recovery. To her credit however, she flatly refused to give her consent for the operation.

She strongly maintained: "If my son is going to die, he's going to die in one piece."

With that said, the matter was never raised again by the medical staff and I began my very slow, agonising recuperation. In the circumstances it was a brave decision for my mother to take but it was one for which, in the years to come, I was eternally grateful.

My first recollections after the accident were of regaining consciousness in a hospital side ward with the nurse, who later became Sister McClean, speaking softly to me with reassuring understatement.

She told me: "Hello Charles, I'm afraid you've had an a bit of an accident."

On reflection I have no doubt it was as a consequence of her professional skill and limitless patience that I eventually made a good recovery.

As the realisation dawned on me where I was, I endeavoured to make some initial tentative body movements, but the effort was to no avail. As I painfully turned my head I saw my right arm was held vice-like, in a metal brace which was at 90 degrees to my chest. My right leg was encased in plaster and the rest of my battered body was tightly surrounded by sausage shaped sandbags to further restrict my movements.

It was at that point the severity of my injuries really hit home and I wondered, with some concern, what my long term recuperation prospects were and if I would be permanently disabled at the tender age of 18.

The orthopaedic specialist treating me was Mr Brittain-Jones, a local man in his late fifties. He was a dedicated doctor to whom I owe a deep debt of gratitude for my eventual recovery. Without his surgical skills and keen personal interest in my case I may well have been permanently disabled for the rest of my life. We were to become great friends during and after my hospitalisation.

Once I had regained consciousness and was out of danger the treatment of my injuries began in earnest. The deep and severe gashes to my right shin, which were so acute they could not be stitched, were a particular source of concern. Apparently they had not been fully treated while I was in a coma in case the shock to my system had caused a relapse in my delicate condition as I hovered precariously for many days between life and death.

When they eventually began treating my injured leg the pain was excruciating. In fact it became so severe and intolerable at times, that often three or four members of the nursing staff had to hold me down on the bed because I was crying out in so much agony.

The main worry of the medical staff was that my leg would become infected and complicate my recovery. So, to counteract that possibility, my extensive lacerations were stripped every other day with what I can only describe as a red hot match which literally burnt the flesh along my shin to deter any infection. Although my leg eventually made a complete recovery I have never forgotten the intense level of pain I to endure before the doctors decided to discontinue the agonising treatment.

Lying unconscious in bed for such a long time took its toll on my physical condition. I lost over four stones in weight and for someone who had been a very active happy go lucky youth, enjoying all sports, particularly playing football for the school and South Bank East End and boxing with the Territorial Army, to find myself in such an emaciated state was indeed both a distressing and depressing experience.

At that point in my life sago pudding suddenly became an important ingredient in my recovery. It was the first semi-solid food I ate after regaining consciousness and because of my physical incapacity I had to be spoon fed by the nursing staff.

For one meal I devoured over 20 small bowls of the stuff and when the nurses jokingly complained to Mr Brittain-Jones about the quantity of my eating habits he cheerfully remarked:

" If it's sago pudding he wants it's sago pudding he'll have. Just feed him."

Slowly I began to recover and after three months in total isolation I was transferred onto a main ward. The house doctor on the ward was a Dr. McClean. A talented amateur footballer he played outside right for South Bank and later became the husband of the nursing sister who had taken such good care of me when I'd first arrived in hospital.

I was grateful for that change of scenery because being on my own was like serving a prison sentence in solitary confinement. To be in the company of other patients again was not only very stimulating, as I could now enter into conversations, but it also provided me with a certain degree of psychological reassurance because it meant - in the opinion of the medical staff - I was definitely making some significant progress.

It was also while I was on the main ward I became familiar with North Ormesby Hospital's infamous unwritten fresh air policy.

At the far end of our ward there were some double doors which opened outwards on to a small terrace, providing pleasant views of the surrounding well-stocked gardens. Even in the depths of winter those doors were fully opened to enable the patients, the majority of whom were confined to bed, to be wheeled out on to the terrace in order to inhale the healthy and invigorating Teesside air to aid their recovery. Unfortunately the policy often defeated its prime objective because most of the recipients regularly ended up with crimson noses and mild hypothermia. It's a wonder we all survived such Arctic conditions.

North Ormesby Hospital, Middlesbrough, where thanks to the devoted skills of the medical staff I defied all the odds and recovered from a serious motorbike accident.

To further facilitate my recovery I also had electrode stimulation treatment three times a week. That process involved placing my arm in a lead lined bath which contained about six inches of water, while an electric current was passed down my arm from a pad attached to my shoulder. The warm sensation was not unpleasant but it didn't appear to have any perceivable effect on restoring the feeling or movement to my arm.

Then one day, during his rounds, Mr Brittain-Jones told me the inevitable news for which I had been steeling myself. He informed me that my right arm had not responded to any of the intensive stimulation treatment I'd been undergoing and unfortunately it would, in all probability, remain limp and lifeless.

Taking his time, he described to me in minute detail how the nerves in my upper arm had been severed in the accident and without their impulses delivering messages to the muscles, my arm would be permanently in a sling. Being a compassionate man he apologised and said that medically there was nothing more he could do for me but he would still monitor my progress as an out-patient.

From a personal point of view, I could cope with the grim medical prognosis because it had not come as a complete surprise to me. I'd realised for quite a while that there was no discernable sensation returning to my arm. But what I did find very disconcerting was the acute emotional over reaction of others towards my predicament.

The well-intentioned commiserations I'd received in hospital directly after the accident, which were initially a source of mild embarrassment, now developed into a stream of melancholic, hand wringing concern. I could understand people were genuinely worried about my long term welfare but as a person who has always had difficulty in verbally conveying my inner feelings to others, the whole experience began to have a deeply harrowing effect on me, particularly when it appeared likely I would be permanently disabled.

In fact that difficult period in my life was to be an emotional watershed. I found it exceedingly hard to come to terms with friends and close relatives constantly consoling me. So much so I became very withdrawn and unable to face people.

My father, endeavouring to aid my convalescence, bought me an Alsatian dog which I named Troy and when I was able to walk again I would escape to the sanctuary of the Eston Hills, near Middlesbrough, and roam for hours with my canine companion to avoid the repeated inquests regarding my physical well-being.

I don't think I've ever fully recovered from the physical and psychological trauma of the accident. My character and personality changed from being a totally carefree, outgoing and active teenager to an individual who was much more conservative, reserved and shy.

Everything I have achieved in later life has been accomplished in spite of the repercussions of the accident and I am personally very proud of those achievements.

Ten months after the crash I was served with a summons to appear at South Bank magistrates court on a charge of dangerous driving. The police sergeant who delivered the letter to our house in Grangetown was very apologetic saying, while he acknowledged and understood the physical and mental ordeal I'd gone through, the undeniable plain facts of the situation were that the insurance companies needed to establish liability for the accident. That would enable them to finally settle the claim of the poor chap whose car I'd apparently written off.

The accident was of course totally my fault and in court I had no option but to plead guilty. I was fined two guineas (two pounds ten pence) with ten shillings (fifty pence) costs. As the verdict was pronounced the chairman of the bench wished me luck and hoped I'd make a good recovery from my injuries, which I thought was a pleasant parting gesture.

I received no insurance money as a result of the accident and at my parents' insistence the offending motorbike was sold for two sovereigns (two pounds).

As an out-patient I still returned to hospital three times a week for electrolysis treatment to try and stimulate some feeling into my right arm. After one of those sessions, which I felt were quite frankly becoming a waste of time, Mr Brittain-Jones asked me to come and see him with my mother and father. As we went into his consulting room I negatively thought he was going to discontinue my ineffective treatment as it appeared to be serving no useful purpose. However to my total surprise what he did say provided me with a faint glimmer of hope for the future.

Coming straight to the point he asked me whether I would like to be a guinea pig. I tentatively enquired for what, and he began to carefully explain to us the details of an experimental operation he was proposing to perform. In fact it was a pioneering procedure which had not been widely attempted in England at that time.

The revolutionary surgical technique involved suturing the severed nerves in the upper part of my arm back together in the hope that over time they may knit together sufficiently to allow some impulses to be conveyed from my brain to the dormant limb.

Brittain-Jones felt sure that because I was so young and had displayed such admirable determination and courage to recover from my injuries, it was a risk worth taking.

Naturally we all agreed to the operation because I was ready and willing to try anything, experimental or not, to restore some feeling to my lifeless arm.

Technically the four hour operation, performed at North Ormesby Hospital, was an unqualified success but Mr Brittain-Jones warned me afterwards that any feeling which might return - and he emphasised the words might return - wouldn't happen for months, possibly even years later. The way I looked at it, however, was that even with the most pessimistic prognosis there was at least a slim chance of an improvement and that was better than none at all.

So innovative and revolutionary was my operation in the early 1930's, that the surgical procedures used were fully published in the highly esteemed medical journal The Lancet for other doctors around the world to read and analyse the methodology.

After the operation, I became good friends with Mr Brittain-Jones and frequently visited him at his house in The Avenue in Middlesbrough so he could continue to monitor my progress. I was, you might say, his star patient and we found during our conversations that we had a mutual passion for music.

I didn't come from a particularly musical background, which is quite surprising because before he arrived to work on Teesside, first in the pay offices at the Eston Mines and then as an engineer at the Bolckow/Vaughan Steelworks in Grangetown, my father had lived with his family in South Wales.

You would have thought being surrounded by all those Welsh male voice choirs should have left some impression on him, but no, the only music in our house was provided by my mother who could play the piano proficiently. My father was, however, a gifted mathematician and my own interest in figures and engineering was probably derived from his attributes.

From an early age I vividly remember loving most music, particularly religious music, which is quite perverse because I'm not a religious person. I often attended the local St. Mary's Catholic Church for the Sunday Mass spoken in Latin by the priest, Father Kelly, to listen to the tempo of the Gregorian Chants which I found deeply atmospheric and very moving.

Then in the afternoon I would go to the Methodist chapel and listen to my father's sister Edith, who married the well known local trade union leader Harry Douglass, later to become Lord Douglass of Cleveland, sing in her distinctive contralto voice while I enthusiastically helped to pump the organ bellows.

The arm injuries resulting from my accident also meant I was unable to hold and play the violin which one of my uncles had given me for my 12th birthday. I was, however, pleasantly surprised to discover not only was my specialist an outstanding surgeon but he was also a more than capable violinist. I spent many an enjoyable evening listening to him play classical music and I'm sure those dulcet interludes aided my recovery.

Following the accident my arm was supported by a sling which meant it was not practically possible for me to return to any of the previous positions I had held. Like so many other Grangetown lads of that era I'd left school at 15 and began work in the local steelworks, earning 8s 6d a week as an office boy in the wages department. However I soon discovered some of my contemporaries were earning 27s 6d in the 18 inch steel mill, so I left the office and almost trebled my income by working in the rolling mill.

I even enquired about a job at the Middlesbrough Evening Gazette and was encouraged to reapply when I could take shorthand and type. Whether they didn't expect me to take a crash course in shorthand I do not know but when I returned to the Gazette Offices for a formal interview I was told it was unlikely that I would be appointed because I didn't have any relations already working for the paper. I was so disappointed after all my hard work, and in fact I was almost in tears as I left the building. It was upsetting to discover that such a discriminatory criteria was being used to fill the newspaper's vacancies.

Although my natural inclination was now to steer clear of those over sympathetic people previously mentioned, I must gratefully acknowledge the constructive contribution made by one person in particular. The admirable Colonel Douglas, the commander of Lytton St. Territorial Army in Middlesbrough who, despite my incapacity, invited me to continue my active involvement with the local platoon. That was a generous gesture because I was treated as one of the lads again and did not have to feel nervous about my injury. In fact my reintroduction to the T.A. routine and lifestyle certainly helped boost my confidence and self-esteem.

I'd joined the T.A. at 16 and learnt how to be gun layer at Catterick Camp in North Yorkshire. I really enjoyed both the discipline and camaraderie and I had many happy, often hilarious, experiences on manoeuvres.

One episode in particular I can recall happened when we were practising firing our guns out to sea at Carnoustie in Scotland.

I was a member of the horse drawn artillery D gun (4.5") battery and after we had successfully completed our firing routine we stood down to watch B gun perform. Their technique, it has to be said, was not as proficient as ours and stumbling through the loading process they somehow calculated their angle of elevation wrongly and when the command to fire was given the trajectory of their live shell was too high. As the missile sailed out to sea it became apparent, much to the consternation of the officer in charge, that local shipping was in danger of becoming an unexpected target. Somewhat fortuitously for the battery members no direct hits were achieved.

At the time there was a deep sense of shock at the disaster which could have befallen B gun. Such as "Local fishing trawler sunk by friendly fire " headlines in the newspapers. But with the retelling of the story over a few drinks in the bar afterwards, the episode became firmly etched into T.A. folklore.

The area of Tayside where we were stationed was also famous for its championship golf courses such as Carnoustie and often the lads from our battery would earn extra money by caddying for the members and guests of the Barry Links Club which was near our camp. On one particular occasion in the mid 1930s I had the privilege of watching Edward, The Prince of Wales, play and he appeared to be a very keen and more than capable golfer.

Being in a horse drawn gun battery I learnt to ride and found I had natural affinity with the animals in my care. They seemed to respond to my attention. That was an important bond to make because when the guns were being transported to their required destination it was vital the horses worked as an obedient team to avoid mishaps.

I remember one particular night when our tough and uncompromising sergeant major, Tocker Gordon, had detailed me for sentry duty from midnight to four in the morning. All was very quite except for the occasional movement of the 40 or so horses tied up on roped lines. Towards the end of my watch, my mind was beginning to wander when I suddenly became aware that I was not alone. Something warm and soft touched my shoulder and I froze. As I slowly plucked up the courage to turn around I was confronted by a large dark shape with steaming nostrils. I've never jumped so high in all my life, until I realised the misty apparition was a loose horse which had quietly padded over to me as if to report its own predicament. As I led the wayward animal back to the line, I thought my pounding heart was going to escape from my chest. What a fright it had given me.

After the accident I particularly enjoyed going away to camp. The whole experience was very therapeutic and always gave a me a very positive psychological lift. It was on one of those T.A. excursions in Scotland a minor miracle happened.

A group of the lads had arranged an excursion to the fishing port of Aberdeen and as we were walking down Union Street my behaviour suddenly gave my companions great cause for concern. Without warning I started leaping up and down shouting: " It's tingling, it's tingling, my arm it's tingling."

A fine body of men. I'm pictured with my Territorial Army colleagues in the early 1930's.

I could hardly contain my joy and elation. It was 18 months since the operation and I actually felt as though my right arm was part of me again and not a useless appendage. I was ecstatic.

Mr Brittain-Jones had told me to inform him immediately if there was any positive reaction to the operation, so I returned home on the first available train to personally deliver the wonderful news.

His instant reaction was to share in my unbridled exhilaration. On reflection I think he must have gained a great deal of satisfaction as well as professional prestige from the success of the surgical procedures he had pioneered. I realise I owe him a deep debt of gratitude because without the initial success of that ground breaking surgery, my life would surely have taken a totally different, possibly less accomplished course. I therefore readily acknowledge Mr Brittain-Jones's vital contribution to my prosperous future and that the positive impetus I received after regaining the movement in my arm was immense.

Over the next few months I worked extremely hard on restoring the strength to the wasted muscles in my right arm by lifting weights, engaging in climbing exercises and repeatedly squeezing a small rubber ball in my hand. But although the muscles themselves became much stronger, the actual amount of arm movement I could achieve was still unfortunately very restricted.

Then out of the blue and as a direct result of the article written about my pioneering operation in the Lancet, an offer of further assistance came from an unexpected source. It was an offer which was to have a crucial impact on the next phase of my life.

Around 1933, during one of my periodic appointments with Mr Brittain-Jones, he told me about a communication he'd received from Sir Ambrose Woodall no less (the distinguished doctor to the Royal Family) and a Dr Sidebottom. They explained that they'd read with great interest the report of my operation in the Lancet and were intrigued by my case and wanted to assist with my recovery.

After discussing at length the implications of the unexpected opportunity with Mr Brittain-Jones and my family, I decided to visit the Manor House Hospital, in Golders Green in London, to undergo some tests with those eminent physicians. Once again I came to the logical conclusion that I had nothing to lose and possibly everything to gain from their involvement.

By the end of my initial week's stay, their extremely optimistic prognosis was that they could restore even more movement to my arm if I was prepared to become a long term resident at the hospital.

I was determined to make as full a recovery from my injuries as possible, so without hesitation I accepted the invitation and returned to London a short time later to commence the protracted treatment process. I eventually underwent a further eight operations on my right arm which were conducted primarily to realign the deltoid muscles around my shoulder and give my arm greater freedom of movement. I remained at the Manor House for a total of 53 weeks.

Following each operation I had an intensive course of physiotherapy and gradually I could feel an improvement in my condition as more and more strength and movement returned to my arm.

But as my hospitalisation dragged on and on so did the acute boredom.

Since the accident I'd spent over two years in medical care and it was beginning to take its depressing toll. Even though I had a gramophone on which to play my records - Arthur Tracey's Smoke Gets in Your Eyes was a particular favourite - and books to read, including the bible, they were not enough to occupy my active mind.

In order to stimulate my monotonous daily routine I surreptitiously began to undertake odd jobs around the ward, like making beds and taking patients' temperatures. One day, however, during doctors' rounds my secret moonlighting was discovered by the matron who saw me making a bed. She angrily remonstrated with me and implied my discreet activities could jeopardise my recovery.

However Dr Sidebottom tactfully calmed the situation by suggesting to the matron the physical activity could in fact benefit the muscle strength in my arm and as long as I was sensible, and didn't tire myself, he saw no reason why I couldn't continue with the valuable exercise.

So from that day, until I was formally discharged, I helped the nursing staff with their daily ward routine, eventually displaying an aptitude for folding the bedsheets into " hospital corners", a skill which I can still perform today if required.

One of life's little luxuries for long-stay patients like myself at the Manor House was our Wednesday afternoon excursion to the local hostelry called the Bull and Bush. It was also the well known watering hole for many of the actors and artistes who were appearing in the London West End theatres and shows. One particular afternoon my fellow orthopaedic patients and I were playing darts - since the accident I'd taught myself to throw quite proficiently with my left hand - when a voice at my back enquired: "Any chance of a game? "

I looked round and there to my surprise was the famous singer/composer Ivor Novello and his friends who were performing at the Golders Green Hippodrome asking us for a game of darts. Of course we said 'yes'. And I must say what a pleasant and personable man he was. No airs or graces, just completely natural, and we passed many an enjoyable Wednesday afternoon in his company.

During my enforced stay at the Manor House I had the privilege of meeting some of the most eminent men of that period who at various times were treated on my ward. They included Cumberland landowner and accomplished sportsman Lord Hugh Lonsdale, who since 1909 had presented belts to the British Boxing Champions, Herbert Morrison, the Labour MP and Home Secretary, and WH Strawbridge, the chairman of the National Council of Labour Colleges.

I particularly enjoyed the evenings when we would all gather around a patient's bed and discuss the burning social issues of the day. Although I must admit I used to do more listening than talking, just to absorb the knowledgeable conversation of those wise and learned men was a unique experience for me.

One particular evening I had not contributed a great deal to a discussion about the Salvation Army when WH Strawbridge turned to me and said: "

You haven't got a lot to say for yourself tonight Charles? " To which I replied rather bluntly: "No sir. I find it's better not to say anything on a subject about which you know very little."

Strawbridge laughed at my forthright answer, replying: "Charles, by adopting that principle in your life you'll certainly go far."

As it turned out, that was quite a prophetic piece of advice in the light of my later success in business.

Although WH Strawbridge was a distinguished academic, I found him to be very approachable and generous with both his time and advice. He even suggested I should join the Labour Party but I've never been that interested in politics, local or national. However I was cajoled into standing for the local council in Redcar in the 1960s. I lost very narrowly, which was an extremely surprising result because I did no canvassing at all.

After one particular late night conversation when I had spoken about the tedium I was experiencing in hospital, Strawbridge suggested I undertake some academic study via a correspondence course. I'd always had an aptitude for working with figures at primary school in Grangetown and later at Coatham Grammar in Redcar, so with his help I enrolled to undertake a course in History and Economics through Ruskin College, Oxford, which I continued after I was discharged from hospital. There is no doubt in my mind, following that programme of study in economics helped to develop my future business career.

After more than 12 months at the Manor House I was finally discharged. It was 1935 and to my delight all the operations and strenuous physiotherapy I'd endured resulted in me having about 95% of the movement back in arm.

Once again I must formally record how indebted I was to the medical profession for their devoted work in helping my recovery which took four full years of treatment. I was also very glad to dispense with the black sling which had provided my arm with support. Not having to wear it as a visible symbol of my injury gave me a massive psychological boost.

I returned to Middlesbrough and after a succession of unrewarding office jobs, which I felt were leading me nowhere, I decided to become self employed. That was probably the most crucial personal decision I have ever made in my entire life. I would be in charge of my own destiny.

Why did I need my independence and why couldn't I settle down to a steady job working for somebody else ?

Without becoming too self analytical, I feel subconsciously I was reacting to the resultant traumas of my accident. I developed an inward determination to prove, not only to myself, but to all those well meaning people who'd been very sympathetic during my recovery that, in spite of my injuries, I still could be a successful individual. So with the moral and financial support of my mother and father I purchased a Liverpool Victoria and Commercial Union insurance round from one of the local agents.

Acquiring the business proved to be very a lucrative venture indeed as it covered the whole of Teesside and served many clients. Initially I tried to do the round on a pushbike but found it was a physical impossibility because I was worn out peddling frantically around the area in all sorts of weather. So I invested the grand sum of £15 and bought my first car, which was a Standard Nine.

Eventually I consolidated the round by selling off the peripheral areas such as Billingham and Stockton and I concentrated my efforts in Middlesbrough on collecting fees for doctors and dentists at sixpence a week. At that time there was no free National Health Service and all medical treatment had to be paid for.

Collecting fees, particularly from households with large families, could have led to misunderstandings between collector and client but I endeavoured to be personable and attempted to cultivate a pleasant and amiable doorstep manner. I worked on the principle that some payment was better than none at all and that business method was to prove very successful, as I developed and fostered a trusting relationship with the local community.

During that period of my life I certainly acquired some of the financial and social skills which would benefit me in my future business career. But I also realised there would be no substitute for hard work if I wished to succeed. That philosophy was vividly brought home to me when I was collecting some insurance premiums in Dormanstown on the outskirts of Middlesbrough. It was there I observed at first hand, the tough and laborious lives of the people who, although existing on small wages, still managed to provide a caring and safe home environment for their children.

One memorable incident poignantly illustrates the work ethic when I suggested to a client, who was expecting a baby, that for an extra penny a week the child would also be covered by her current insurance policy.

A few months later I arrived at the house to find the new addition to the family sleeping contentedly in a cot and the revised amount of two shillings for the insurance premium placed on the mantelpiece. I congratulated her on the fine healthy baby and enquired when it had been born. I was totally unprepared for the reply I received and could only listen in utter disbelief to the calm explanation which followed.

Apparently the baby had been delivered at two-thirty that morning in an upstairs bedroom. But by ten-thirty the mother was up and about doing the weekly wash by hand. I was amazed at the matter of fact way in which she recounted the story and how she prioritised her life. Childbirth seemed to be a minor interference in the daily grinding routine of living in 1930s Dormanstown.

That incident left an indelible mark in my mind. It was a shining example of hard work and dedication in practise, and one which I would never forget.

CHAPTER TWO

Hi-Di-Hi

By the mid 1930s I was physically much improved, so I rekindled my interest in music by playing saxophone in a small dance band which included a friend of mine, Charlie Skinner on violin. I organised evening functions under the title of the Troubadours for no other reason than I simply liked the name. We toured the smaller local dance halls on Teesside like the Co-op Hall South Bank and Carlin How Working Men's Institute and by 1936 we'd built up quite a loyal following.

Eventually I began to promote my own larger charity dances on behalf of the Red Cross and St John Ambulance Brigade. I endeavoured to book the best bands in the area, such as Jack Marwood and his Orchestra, and that carefully calculated strategy ensured me the good attendances which I was seeking.

I specifically chose medical organisations to be the recipients of my initial charity work because I wanted to say a deep felt thank-you to the profession for all the care and attention I'd received during the long, and sometimes painful recovery period from my motorbike accident. In fact I still have a letter from James Meaburn, the divisional secretary of the St John Ambulance Brigade, thanking me for donating the proceeds of one of my very first dances to his organisation.

My fledgling career as a promoter was developing steadily when one night at Carlin How I noticed, after about 15 minutes of playing to a full house of over 250 young people, there were only three couples actually on the dance floor. The rest were evenly split with the girls on one side of the hall and the lads on the other. In fact some of the lads were so shy they were pretending to read the local Evening Gazette. Rather perplexed by the apparent lack of interest in our music, I turned to one of the locals, a Mr. Robinson and asked: "What's the matter with them, don't they like the band?"

" The band's fine," he replied. " It's just most of them can't dance."

I had to laugh out loud because I hadn't bargained for that eventuality. I'd naively presumed the only prerequisite required for a successful social evening was for the band to turn up and play. It had never occurred to me for one minute that the audience wouldn't be able to dance and their none participation rather defeated the object of the evening's entertainment.

The solution to the problem was simple and quite straight forward. My wife and I decided to give an hour's tuition prior to every dance commencing.

We'd been taught all the basic dance steps by a very competent tutor from South Bank and we were by then proficient enough to teach absolute beginners. In fact it was at Phil Whitcombe's dance studio where I'd first met Margaret before we were eventually married at St John's Church in South Bank.

To cover the cost of our tuition we added sixpence to the entrance charge and in all honesty we only expected a few interested youngsters to enrol. But how wrong we were. Right from the beginning the classes proved immensely popular and at every venue we regularly had attendances of over 100 novices trying to come to terms with the vagaries of the fox-trot and the waltz.

In those days being able to dance was seen as a social necessity and a way of meeting people, particularly the opposite sex, so if you wanted to make a favourable impression you had to exhibit some fancy footwork on the dance floor. During the course of those beginners classes I found I was both a competent and confident teacher with a capacity to organise and relate to people. It was to be those same communication skills which I was to put to good use as my career in the entertainment business flourished in the years to come.

In 1937 a family bereavement, coupled with my own keenly developed sense of curiosity, was to dramatically change the course of my whole life.

My grandfather, Frederick Porter, unfortunately died at the ripe old age of 93. He had led a very colourful and chequered life and among his numerous and diverse occupations he had been a hotelier in Barnard Castle, County Durham, and a sheep farmer in Australia.

In order to discuss the details of my grandfather's estate my parents had to visit a firm of solicitors in Louth.

*Margaret and I, not on a slow boat to China,
but enjoying the delights of Bridlington boating lake.*

As a child I'd visited my relations on their fertile Lincolnshire potato farm many times during the summer holidays, enjoying my own company in the peace and tranquility of the Fen countryside near Boston. They were marvellous idyllic times where I could literally lean out of my bedroom window and pick apples and pears from the abundance of fruit trees which grew close to the house.

Unfortunately due to the motorbike accident my memory is often fitful when trying to recount the precise events of my early childhood spent in the tightly knit community of Grangetown but I can honestly say some of the happiest moments of my life occurred when I was staying on the farm.

One incident I do vividly remember happened after I'd caught an eel while fishing. I rushed back to the farm to share my angling success and in my eagerness and excitement to locate the adults I placed my prize catch on the kitchen table.

When I proudly returned to the kitchen with my great aunt, we arrived just in time to see the tail end of the eel disappearing into the mouth of a grateful and contented large farmhouse cat. It was probably the freshest fish meal it had ever eaten, but that was the last thing on my mind as I chased the feline thief out into the yard for stealing my moment of glory.

Those were pleasant carefree days when I was quite content to create my own amusement. I actually enjoyed the solitude and to some extent I always have done. I think deep down I must be a loner at heart.

After my grandfather's death I drove my parents to their appointment with the solicitors but I must confess I did have an ulterior motive for doing so. I wanted to visit the East Coast resort of Skegness and reconnoitre a new and completely original leisure development called a Butlins Holiday Camp, which had been vigorously advertised at the time in the local Teesside press.

As I approached the entrance barrier to the expansive camp development one sunny June afternoon I was stopped by an amiable and immaculately dressed commissionaire who informed me from the window of his wooden booth that the camp was unfortunately closed to visitors. Instantly and without hesitation I confidently replied that I had an appointment with the entertainments manager. After a quick telephone call he surprisingly raised the barrier and even obligingly pointed me in the general direction of the camp's management offices.

Once inside the offices I continued the cloak and dagger charade by duplicating the same bogus story to the young receptionist. I was informed the person in question wouldn't be available for about 20 minutes, so it was suggested I strolled around the very impressive on-site facilities which were surrounded by pleasantly manicured landscaped lawns.

Skegness was Bill Butlin's first luxury holiday camp and had opened to the public on Easter Sunday, 1936. Initially it accommodated over 1,000 campers in 600 chalets, all with electricity and running water. The camp also boasted dining and recreation halls, a theatre, gymnasium, a rhododendron-bordered swimming pool with cascades at either end and a boating lake. The many purpose built sporting facilities included tennis courts, bowling and putting greens, cricket pitches and a running track.

As I wandered around the camp I must admit I felt somewhat over dressed and rather conspicuous in my suit and tie, while surrounded by people attired in leisure wear and red coats.

I was, however, immediately struck by the friendly atmosphere and cheery disposition of both the campers and the staff. It was obvious all the residents were having a carefree time. It was a holiday format which was clearly working and even after such a short time I decided there and then that the camp was a unique and exciting innovation and one with considerable future potential.

When I entered the office of the Director of Entertainments, Norman Bradford, he said bluntly:

"I haven't got a meeting with you have I?"

"No I'm afraid you haven't," I replied rather apologetically. "I concocted the story in the hope of seeing you."

"Then why are you here?" came back the rather stern enquiry.

I half expected to be quickly shown the door for wasting his time but surprisingly he allowed me to outline my reasons for gatecrashing the camp. I explained that the North-eastern press reports about Butlin's Skegness were very positive and complimentary indeed and that some of my insurance clients who had stayed at the camp were astounded that their holiday had been such good value for money. At between 35 shillings and £3 for three meals a day all in, they'd had a wonderful time. And the added bonus was that it didn't even matter about the notorious British summer weather, because the free indoor entertainment kept the whole family amused, rain or shine.

As my observations seemed to be much appreciated, I then proceeded to emphasise how very impressed I'd been with what I'd seen of the camp's facilities and that I had some relevant experience in the entertainment business as I was now promoting my own successful dances in the Teesside area.

The impromptu explanation and compliments, not to mention the bare faced cheek of brazenly walking into his office, must have made a positive impression on Norman Bradford because he surprisingly offered me a position on the entertainments staff on the spot.

Trying to remain calm, but inwardly feeling overjoyed, I asked when he needed a reply to the job offer.

"End of the week do?" he suggested.

"Fine," I said, while at the same time wondering what on earth was I going to tell Margaret, and what about the insurance round?

I knew for certain that a large window of personal opportunity had just been opened. Bill Butlin had created a highly original business which greatly appealed to me and I wanted to become part of it. As it turned out Margaret was very supportive, as she has been all through our marriage when it comes to my business interests. She quite rightly stressed the position I'd been offered was too good to miss and she would take charge of the insurance round.

With that arrangement in place I was able to return to Skegness for the last two months of the 1937 summer season to familiarise myself with the camp organisation and to meet the colleagues with whom I'd be working.

My newly created appointment at Skegness, for the princely weekly salary of three pounds ten shillings, was assistant to the entertainments manager, the amiable and hardworking Frank Cusworth. My initial responsibility was to help with the training of the famous Butlin Redcoats and because of my dance hall experience I was also instructed to announce the variety acts on to the stage in the evening.

That high profile contact quickly enabled me to cultivate an essential rapport with the holidaymakers, many of whom were experiencing their first " real " holiday and were determined to enjoy themselves to the full.

At the end of their stay it was quite common for the campers to present the entertainment staff with small gifts such as watches and silver cigarette cases as tokens of their appreciation. It was as a result of those generous gifts I began to take an interest in collecting silver and over the years I have accumulated some fine pieces.

The overall scale of the holiday operation at Butlin's Skegness was enormous and in order for the camp to function efficiently everything had to be organised with supreme military style precision.

It was basically a co-ordinated exercise in logistics. On a Saturday, which was changeover day, we handled thousands of campers, most of whom arrived and departed to and from Skegness railway station in a fleet of coaches.

I once saw some enlightening statistics relating to a typical Butlin's holiday camp before World War Two. At any given time during high season there could be upwards of 5,000 people on site every week. They were all fed three times a day in the massive dining halls consuming a total of four tons of potatoes every 24 hours and the weekly supply of 10,000 bed sheets and pillow cases was enough to cover an airport runway. Thousands of items of crockery and cutlery were either broken, lost or damaged but undoubtedly many of those were purloined as souvenirs because the cutlery was engraved with the Butlin's name. Bill Butlin was, however, rather philosophical about the pilfering, regarding the losses as a cheap form of holiday advertising.

A wide variety of entertainment and activities tailored to suit every generation, region or country (the Scots and the Irish often had their own separate weekly block bookings) also had to be provided day and night regardless of the weather.

When the Skegness camp first opened in 1936 the evening entertainment was very haphazard and provided by pressganged staff volunteers or some of the talentless campers. But a year later when I joined Butlin's, top class artistes were performing in our own well equipped theatre.

The dramatic change occurred when Bill Butlin, ever the innovator, asked a show business agent what his variety acts did on Sundays. The answer was that most of them were either travelling between engagements or were resting. He then enquired if any of them would consider working for him over the weekend and the reaction was very favourable.

In no time at all the first Sunday Night Celebrity Concert was staged at Skegness, starring the famous female impersonator of that era, Norman Evans, performing his "over the garden wall" monologues. It was a resounding success and from then on the Butlin name gained a reputation for not only providing great value holidays but it also became synonymous with top quality variety entertainment.

That new and exciting development in entertainment served to entice even more willing customers to the camp. There was also the added bonus of the free publicity from the thousands of postcards sent home each week by the campers to their envious friends containing information about the big name stars they'd seen for free in the Butlin's theatre. The Butlin showbiz revolution was well under way and gathering momentum.

In the late 1930s and 1940s television was still in its infancy so the stars of the day could only be heard on the radio or seen at either the cinema or theatre. Bill Butlin was again quick to spot a potential gap in the market by marrying his captive weekly audience with the popular celebrities of the entertainment world who, in their turn, were only too pleased to perform for such highly enthusiastic and appreciative large audiences.

Guest appearances were made before and after World War Two by a wide range of famous stars including Elsie and Doris Waters, Ted Ray, Will Hay, Harry Champion, Donald Peers, Tommy Handley, Richard Murdoch, Kenneth Horne and Arthur Askey.

Mantovani's Tipica Orchestra and the big bands of Lew Stone and Billy Thornburn became resident attractions in the camp ballrooms, while many of the top sporting personalities like outstanding boxers Jimmy Wilde and Len Harvey, cricketer Len Hutton and snooker players Joe Davis and Horace Lindrum were either frequent visitors or resident for a full season.

Being very interested in boxing I once asked the great flyweight world champion Jimmy Wilde, who eventually went to the United States to fight because he'd beaten all the credible opposition in Europe, how he managed to knockout so many opponents who were often twice his size. His reply was simple. There was no great secret or mystery, it was all down to timing the punches with precision. Wilde also felt timing was an innate skill which could not be taught in the gym.

Although those big name personalities and celebrities certainly did much to publicise and promote the camps, Bill Butlin always had one eye on the next season's bookings and made sure most of the visits were prominently featured in the main national newspapers.

The daily responsibility for camp entertainment was the duty of the now famous Butlin Redcoats and the story of their creation is very interesting but it left much to chance.

According to Skegness legend, in 1936 Bill Butlin's natural intuition sensed some vital element was missing from the camp atmosphere during its inaugural week. The campers were not utilising the facilities as much as he'd envisaged and they were not mixing with each other. In short, there was a distinct lack of camaraderie and bonhomie. The problem was eventually identified as the campers possibly being too self conscious in the new type of social environment.

In an effort to resolve the predicament Norman Bradford was instructed to "liven them up a bit". He went on stage in his usual jovial manner and completely of the cuff suggested the campers should turn to the person next to them, smile, shake hands and introduce themselves. Initially there was an outbreak of understandable red faced embarrassment at his request, but as soon as some of the more gregarious campers began to carry out the instructions, the ice was immediately broken and the whole atmosphere in the camp relaxed overnight.

Bill Butlin then quickly realised that voluntary participation was to be the important key element in the ultimate success of his camps. A wider choice of more structured activities had to be provided and organised by a highly motivated and committed entertainment staff. For that specific purpose he chose ten personable members of staff, five lads and five girls, kitted them out in distinctive coloured blazers and slacks, and the result was the famous Redcoats.

Billingham born redcoat Jackie Clancy MM, discusses the entertainment programme with an attentive Bill Butlin and myself at Filey in 1946.

Being a Redcoat was a high profile and demanding full-time position. It required the blazer wearer to be constantly amiable, friendly and patient, day and night, and believe me that was not always easy when you were confronted with some of the holidaymakers' antics.

Redcoats also had to be multi-talented individuals, possessing the ability to switch easily from singing and dancing with senior citizens in the ballroom, to organising the children's donkey derby. They always had to be seen to be enjoying themselves, the theory being that their infectious enthusiasm would be transmitted to the campers.

The whole Redcoat concept was an example of a simple idea which worked well in practice. And even though it was an extremely tiring job, with long hours, we were always inundated with applications for any vacant positions which arose.

Sound planning and meticulous organisation were important to the smooth running of the camp and early morning meetings were held in the entertainment manager's office to establish the running order of daily events. They often had to be flexible to take into account the unpredictable nature of the British summer weather, but as we became more experienced we were able to establish a structured weekly roster of events, displayed on a wall chart in the office, based on their popularity with the campers. That visual aid enabled the entertainment staff to plan more accurately in advance just when and where, and in what numbers, the Redcoats would be required for specific activities.

For the duration of their stay, in order to foster a sense of team spirit, the campers were assigned to a house, for example York or Windsor, and given a distinguishing badge to cement their membership and thus create a feeling of belonging. Every house had a Redcoat captain who organised voluntary teams to participate against other houses in football, cricket, swimming, tug of war etc. The results of those good natured challenge matches were all collated at the end of the week and the victorious participants were given a memento to take home with them.

Over the years there seems to have been a general misconception about Butlin's Holiday Camps, mostly initiated by people who had never actually been to one, that the campers were somehow cajoled or browbeaten into participating in the activities. That was simply not true. I've always felt those accusations were grossly exaggerated, particularly when for the six years during World War Two the lives of the whole population had revolved around conformity and regimentation. As a result of that routine experience, people most certainly would not have accepted being organised while they were away on holiday.

It must therefore be emphasised that the activities were provided for all generations on a purely voluntary basis and the campers could opt in and out, wherever and whenever they wished to do so. In fact it was quite possible for campers to have an enjoyable holiday by simply watching others' wacky exploits or by being very selective with their own involvement. There was no pressure to participate. The campers just reacted to the carefree atmosphere.

One of the traditional weekly organised events was the staff versus campers cricket match which was usually played in fancy dress. For one particular fixture I was wearing a rather fetching Victorian lady's costume which had a heavily reinforced circular underskirt. Not what you might call the ideal type of sporting attire in which to bowl, field or score runs.

The staff duly lost the match and as was the established custom at Butlin's all the losing team were thrown fully clothed into the swimming pool. As I was catapulted into the deep end by the jubilant victors I quickly realised I was not returning to the surface. In fact the sensation I experienced was quite the reverse. The problem was that the bell shaped dress which I was wearing retained a great weight of water and caused me to sink to the bottom of the pool. After a few seconds I began to panic, when I realised the seriousness of my predicament.

As the time passed, in what appeared to be slow motion, I tried unsuccessfully to thrash my way up to the surface. Eventually my non-appearance must have created some alarm because just as I thought I might drown, I suddenly felt the strong hands of the entertainments manager Frank Cusworth hoist me up to safety and glorious fresh air. Needless to say, after such a sobering experience, I always wore something more appropriate with which to enter the pool.

When I first joined the entertainments staff at Butlins in the middle of the 1937 season my complexion was very pale and wan in comparison to the suntanned skins of the other Redcoats, who had been working at the camp since the spring. In fact with my lily white legs and arms I stood out like a flashing neon light. It was all quite embarrassing.

My physical predicament was noticed by the gypsy who was in charge of the riding ponies. He told me if I wanted to quickly cultivate a deep tan, a mixture of black vinegar and sea water liberally applied over my body would do the trick. I was initially quite sceptical about using the strange concoction, but after just one hesitant application and a brief lie in the sun, I looked quite swarthy and gave the appearance of having just spent a month in a Mediterranean resort. The bizarre mixture certainly had the desired effect, as my darker skin tone soon resembled the rest of the entertainments staff and I didn't feel so self-conscious or conspicuous.

The same gypsy also had an unconventional line in medical treatment as I found out when I had a boil on my left forearm. I was due to play in a football match against the campers, in my customary attacking wing half position, but was troubled by an inflammation just below my elbow. The gypsy's solution to my condition was to place a pint bottle filled with hot water over the offending area and press down very hard in order to create a vacuum. Pausing for just a few seconds he then, in one swift movement, wrenched the bottle away from my arm removing the boil and its root.

I'm sure if there'd been a roof above me I would have gone right through it. The individualistic suction treatment certainly did the trick, however, because the swelling never reappeared and I even played in the match with my arm bandaged. The only reminder I have of the incident is a slight skin blemish where the boil had once been.

The wide range of free entertainment and activities provided at the camp was the product of Bill Butlin's very fertile and creative mind. He was always endeavouring to introduce something original into the schedules in order to stimulate and maintain the holidaymaker's interest.

Before World War Two at Skegness, great emphasis was placed on activities with a sporting theme. For example there was a boxing challenge where members of the public could win £5 if they lasted three rounds with the camp champion. The champ was usually one of the tough fairground staff who could handle himself. But to their credit the activity always proved very popular with the campers and there was never any shortage of willing volunteers to "have a go", and some of them actually even survived long enough to take home the money.

Another enjoyable event was the weekly inter-house athletics meeting which was usually held on a Sunday afternoon using the full size track. It included a mixture of standard running races like 100 and 200 yards and in order to cater for all ages and ability levels there were novelty events such as obstacle, egg and spoon and sack.

Hundreds of people at a time also participated in the outdoor keep fit classes on the lawns. To see so many campers of all shapes and sizes exercising in unison was indeed quite a physiological spectacle.

Indoor sports weren't neglected, with snooker and billiards exhibitions provided by those famous amiable brothers Joe and Fred Davis, who always gave the campers the opportunity to test their green baize skills against the experts.

Some of the Bill Butlin's other entertainment innovations were unconventional to say the least and one of the most outrageous was cheetah racing. The basic idea was to release the big cats onto the straight of the running track. They would then run about 100 yards to their handlers who were standing at the finish with some nutritious inducement. The campers were encouraged to predict the outcome of the race, but the spectacle didn't last very long as it was felt the cheetah's behaviour could become too unpredictable and dangerous when subjected to the cheering mass of campers. I must say I was glad to see the stunt shelved because I was only involved with the organisation once and that was enough. I don't mind admitting when I saw those big cats travelling towards me at over 50 miles per hour it scared me half to death.

Musician and comedian "Stanelli", centre, and I in front of the packed athletics track with students from Loughborough College who were on a training course at Skegness.

Another bizarre event, which was a sign of the times and perfectly encapsulated the mood of the pre-war era, was the craze for high diving into shallow tanks of water. At Butlin's we regularly had death defying performers who would plunge from a small platform over 100 feet above the campers into about three feet of flaming water and live to tell the tale. It was a captivating spectacle for the campers, whose audible gasps of horror, as the participants swallow dived through the air to certain oblivion, were replaced by cheers of great relief as they emerged from the smoking tank unscathed. Performing such a spectacular feat in public I have always thought borders on somewhere between the brave and the foolhardy but one had to admire their courage, all in the name of entertainment. It proved to be an extremely popular event indeed.

Pleasure flights in biplanes around the resorts were also an attractive innovation for the campers. The aircraft took off and landed on makeshift runways next to the camps. However, one particular flight at Skegness, just before the War, involving a member of the management team, almost ended in tragedy.

Harold Vinter had taken to the air to experience for himself the thrill of open air flying. Unfortunately, prior to take off, he neglected to secure his safety harness properly and as the pilot engaged in some low level elementary aerobatics, Harold fell out. In normal circumstances, even plunging less than 100 feet would certainly kill you, but Harold was very fortunate indeed when his fall was cushioned by a tree in full foliage.

We still expected him to be at the very least critically injured but as he was extracated from the branches and taken to hospital, it was discovered that he had escaped miraculously with only concussion and severe bruising. Although it is now a very amusing anecdote to recount, the incident had potentially fatal consequences and was an early example of the importance of checking all your safety procedures.

I am pleased to say that Harold made a complete recovery and went on to become one of Bill Butlin's trusted right-hand men.

In contrast to the more eccentric activities we also had the usual weekly standard competitions everybody remembers from Butlin's. No doubt some of you will have participated in such contests as the Bonniest Baby, the Glamorous Granny and the ever popular Knobbliest Knees which were often judged by gently pressganged visiting celebrities who were then pictured with the happy winners to promote Butlin's as the place where the ordinary holiday maker had the opportunity to rub shoulders with the stars.

Rainy days in a holiday camp could often be very grim and depressing, stretching the ingenuity of the entertainments staff in an effort to keep the campers amused with fresh and original activities.

During one particularly inclement week in June, I hastily organised a game of " Housey Housey " in one of the main dance halls. I was absolutely astounded when over two thousand people attended the impromptu activity. The campers were so enthusiastic to participate in the session it was very quickly agreed by the entertainments staff that we should incorporate the event into the weekly itinerary, regardless of the weather. We charged a shilling a card as an entrance fee with a top cash prize amounting to £50, which was a great deal of money before World War Two.

There have been many accusations that Bill Butlin's holidays only pandered to the taste of the working class masses but in those early days I was not personally aware of any snobbery with regard to the camps. We catered for people right across the social spectrum. It was quite common to have both manual and professional families on site in the same week. To the staff they were all equal when they crossed the camp threshold. Skegness was

*A panel of celebrity judges at Filey, left to right,
Billy Boyle, Mantovani, Godfrey Winn and Charles Amer.*

simply a novel holiday concept and the facilities were appreciated by everybody, regardless of any perceived social status.

One of my favourite early camp stories, which emphasises the empathy and feeling of belonging established at Skegness, involved a lady who was asked by Bill Butlin why she was carefully watering the flowering rose tree growing opposite her chalet. In reply, she told him she had no garden at home and for the duration of her holiday she was pretending the tree was her own. Those caring sentiments encapsulated perfectly the atmosphere which proliferated within the camps in those early days.

Although we did have security officers I can recall very few people being asked to leave the camp for breaking the rules. Most of the campers respected the staff and the facilities and valued their holiday time too much to deliberately cause trouble which would lead them to be expelled.

The only real problem I encountered at any camp was when we hosted the party political conference season at Filey in the late 1940s.

If you have ever holidayed at Butlin's you will know the National Anthem was always played to formally conclude the evening's entertainment in the ballroom. At this juncture I have to confess to being a staunch royalist, so I was quite a stickler for continuing the tradition. One particular evening, however, the band found themselves in competition with a few lads, who were more than a little left wing, singing the Red Flag. And the louder they sang, the louder we played to drown out their tuneless glee club.

The following evening, in an attempt to suffocate the National Anthem, reinforcements arrived for their Red Flag rendition but I would not be beaten and the band continued to play as loud as possible. My determined stance led to some threatening behaviour and the altercations even made the pages of the national press, because the leading political journalists of the day were all at the camp covering the conference. The events were reported under the prominent banner headline of " Band leader outplays the Red Flag".

Once the article had been printed I received over 400 letters of support from all around the country backing the stance I'd taken, and to my mind that reaction totally vindicated the position I'd adopted.

The mood of the opposition became even more intimidating when they realised I wasn't going to capitulate under their pressure. In fact the mood degenerated to such an extent that the band were threatened with physical violence if I didn't comply with their wishes.

Group Captain Borthwick-Clarke, the camp controller, in an effort to defuse the rising tension, asked me to stop playing God Save The King but I refused, for the very reasons I've already explained. The solution was eventually provided by Bill Butlin, who had instructed me that under no circumstances was the playing of the National Anthem to be discontinued.

Butlin's early business reputation was initially made on the tough funfairs of England and he was well used to dealing with over enthusiastic customers. To solve our escalating problem he immediately dispatched the services of several robust funfair operators, who stood at the front of the stage to deter any of the audience from disrupting the end of evening proceedings. Funny how the behaviour of many of the antagonists improved once those strapping minders were in residence.

After World War Two Bill Butlin experimented with all manner of entertainment even including the staging of full grand operas by composers like Puccini. There appeared at times to be no star or personality he could not persuade to perform at one of his camps.

Many would-be entertainers were also very quick to realise that working as a Butlin Redcoat could often be their first tentative, but important, step on the showbusiness ladder.

Many familiar television personalities such as Charlie Drake, Benny Hill, Des O'Connor, Larry Grayson, Dave Allen, Ted Rogers, Roy Hudd, Jimmy Tarbuck and Cliff Richard all began their careers in shows like the Redcoats Revue. And I am pleased to say I gave some of them a helping hand on to the ladder of stardom.

Des O'Connor was with me at Filey for a couple of years, just after he'd finished his National Service. He was a very confident and brash individual but his biggest assets were undoubtedly his cheeky grin and dimples. They were to be his passport to fame and fortune.

Des initially had responsibility for the sports and social activities and he also met the new campers in the reception hall every Saturday. He was particularly good with children and organised a game called "Hunt the Pirate" which entailed him being chased around the camp by a marauding band of youngsters, before eventually, and predictably, being caught and thrown fully clothed into the swimming pool.

It was obvious, however, from the beginning of his Butlin career that Des O'Connor had a burning desire to be in showbusiness. He could often be found in and around the theatre when he should have been performing his Redcoat duties elsewhere on site. On more than one occasion he was threatened with the sack. He was repeatedly rejected for the camp show but to his credit he was very persistent about wanting to perform on stage.

I remember one Sunday afternoon during a dance band interval I was sitting having a drink with my band manager, Eric Davison, when we noticed some of the campers attempting to escape from the ear splitting noise which was suddenly emanating from the ballroom. They were complaining that the Redcoat on the microphone was deafening. I sent Eric to investigate the source of the irritation and he found the miscreant was Des O'Connor, who was shouting into the mouthpiece instead of allowing the equipment to project his voice naturally. That lack of basic communication technique was due entirely to his inexperience. Eric quietly removed him from the stage and told him to come and see me the following day in the entertainments office.

During our meeting the persistent Des once again expressed a keen interest in wishing to perform in one of the Sunday concerts. I must admit I was rather reluctant to allow him to perform because he could only sing in one key (nothing has changed) but he did have a very amiable personality which the campers, particularly the ladies, seemed to find appealing. So I followed my instincts and allowed him perform one evening when three of the comics mysteriously called in sick. Butlin rumour has it, however, that their non-appearance and Des O'Connor's debut performance on stage were more than a little coincidental.

Des's act at Filey improved very quickly. He progressed from crib-writing his material on the back of a newspaper to being able to ad-lib his way through a spot. He was eventually noticed by a showbusiness agent who booked him on to the variety hall circuit from where he made the very successful transition into the world of television light entertainment.

I am pleased to see, even after 40 years, he is still presenting his own variety show on TV because it proves I was right to give him professional encouragement. On the other hand some people would say I should share part of the blame for subjecting the country to Des O'Connor!

Around 1946 Charlie Drake was a boxing and jujitsu instructor at Filey. He had boxed for the RAF during the war and at around five foot he was the ideal size to persuade the campers to climb into the ring with him without fear of being knocked out. Charlie was an extremely agile man who clowned around a good deal in the ring. He was a very physical comedian, very much in the same mould as the legendary Charlie Chaplin.

At Filey, Drake struck up a lasting friendship with a 6'3" stage manager called Jack Edwards. I immediately spotted the comic potential of the double act and suggested they should perform together for the campers. They went down a storm with their slapstick routines and the total contrast in their physiques only served to enhance their comedy appeal.

They eventually became the well known double act "Mick and Montmorency" and were signed by the BBC in the 1950s to star in Children's Hour.

Looking rather anxious, I assist Charlie Drake, left, and Jack Edwards, alias Mick and Montmorency, at Filey with one of their hilarious slackstick sketches.

Benny Hill would never have been booked for Butlin's if I'd not personally gone to watch him at a theatre in Scarborough. He was performing his one man show to a very sparse audience and was going down like the proverbial lead balloon. But I thought he had some potential. I found him amusing and his seaside postcard brand of humour provided a contrast to the other Butlin variety acts of that time. I booked him for our Filey shows where he proved to be very popular. Eventually he also made the successful transition into television and films and became one of the nation's favourite and much loved comedians.

Larry Grayson first came to my attention in a small theatre in Redcar near the Coatham Hotel. In those days he was a struggling unknown comic called Billy Breen. But like Benny Hill I felt he had some potential so, after watching his act, I booked him for a Butlin variety show. He later achieved notoriety as a "camp" comedian with catchphrases like "Shut That Door" and "Look At The Muck In Here". He eventually hosted the BBC TV's popular light entertainment programme The Generation Game for a number of years.

Performing in Butlin theatres to a wide cross section of age ranges certainly proved to be a good training ground for budding comedians. Bill Butlin, however, always insisted on clean material being used in his variety shows. There was definitely to be no resorting to blue jokes in order to raise a laugh.

In fact to emphasise that strict rule, a firm directive was posted on some of the dressing room doors which read: "Watch your material! Don't use blue gags because the children don't understand them, their parents don't like them and I'll not have them at any price."

How times have changed. The only way it seems some contemporary comedians can raise a laugh these days is by resorting to the repetitive use of expletives. Call me old fashioned but to my mind that's not humour, it's plain obscenity and has no place in mainstream entertainment.

In those early years before World War Two many innovations and alterations were made to the organisation of the entertainment provided at Skegness. It was a constant learning process for everybody involved.

Often the campers themselves would make practical suggestions which broadened the appeal of the activities. That was the case when a camper called Gladys suggested, even before the days of political correctness, there should be PT classes for ladies as well as men. She was, of course, quite right and because of her obvious enthusiasm we encouraged her to stay on at the camp to become a Redcoat. She later became a games leader under our physical training instructor Captain Bond and was a very successful member of staff.

The most famous example by far of the holidaymakers influencing a camp routine was the adoption of the now legendary chant "Hi-di-Hi! Ho-di-Ho!". It happened quite spontaneously at Skegness after a popular American army film of the time, featuring chanting drill soldiers, was widely shown at British cinemas.

One day the entertainments director Norman Bradford was addressing the campers from the stage when he suddenly shouted out "Hi-di-Hi". Quick as a flash came back the reply "Ho-di-Ho". The practice soon caught on, eventually becoming an indelible part of the Butlin holiday routine. The chant also became the title of a popular long running BBC TV sit-com which parodied, quite accurately in some instances, life in a holiday camp.

There's no doubt in my mind Bill Butlin was a leisure industry visionary. He pioneered and developed the concept of linking holidays and entertainment on one site, at a price people could afford. But even great businessmen need their share of fortune in order to succeed and I'll outline later with regard to my own business career how "lady luck" or, to be more exact, being in the right place at the right time, can determine the success or failure of an embryonic business venture. And it was those same fortuitous factors which were partly instrumental in the early development of the Butlin Holiday Camps.

During the late 1930s very few working people had holidays with pay. But in 1938 a change in the law gave industrial workers the statutory right to an annual paid holiday. That alteration provided the key impetus for the expansion of Bill Butlin's leisure business coupled with the use of catchy advertising slogans tailored to the new legislation, "A week's play for a week's pay, " people flocked in their thousands to the Skegness camp.

The foundations of the Butlin empire were very carefully laid but one must give credit to the rather shy unassuming man who skillfully recognised at that time, a unique business opportunity and maximised it to its fullest potential.

He was also a shrewd, observant man and on his weekly visits to a camp nothing escaped his attention. He dealt ruthlessly with inefficiency and incompetence but also acknowledged and rewarded hard work. His philosophy was, if he worked hard, then it was expected his staff would do likewise. He led by example. I always called him "Guv'nor" even though he preferred his senior staff to call him Bill. I could never have used his first name because I respected him far too much.

My initial personal contact with Bill Butlin occurred in my second season at Skegness, after he'd attended a weekly management meeting. I was standing at one of the camp's crowded milk bars having just ordered my favourite strawberry milkshake. By mistake, I was given the wrong change by the flustered barmaid, so I politely informed her I'd received the change for a shilling instead of a florin by quipping: "Bill Butlin might be a millionaire, but I've got only half his money."

I hadn't got the words out of my mouth when a quiet voice behind me remarked: "I didn't know you had half a million pounds Charles."

I turned around to see who the sarcastic wag was and to my total embarrassment there stood the immaculately dressed figure of Bill Butlin. I had no idea he'd been standing behind me. You could have knocked me down with the proverbial feather. Talk about wishing for the ground to open and swallow you up.

" Well if you've got so much money I'd better let you buy me a milk shake," he suggested with a broad smile on his face.

So I did. It cost me the princely sum of four pence and it was possibly one of the best investments I have ever made in my entire life.

As we chatted he told me he'd heard good reports about my diligent work over the two previous seasons and that my contribution in the ballroom during the evening was very much appreciated and had certainly not gone unnoticed. I was amazed he knew so much about me. In hindsight he was in fact giving me an elementary lesson in how to run a successful business. Firstly, get to know your staff. It was an impromptu tutorial and one I would remember during my own future business career.

The Guv'nor then proceeded to explain that Frank Cusworth was having to spend more and more time on site development and camp expansion and was finding it increasingly difficult to fulfil the important role of entertainments manager. He was therefore offering me the prominent position, if I was interested.

I needed no second invitation and accepted the offer without a moment's thought. I felt a great sense of achievement because my promotion to the inner management team entrusted me with more responsibility and the opportunity to constructively influence the camp's decision making process.

Bill Butlin was also a very kind and generous man who anonymously gave substantial donations to charity and he was instrumental in providing some of the initial funding required to inaugurate the successful Duke of Edinburgh Outward Bound Award Scheme.

I also remember very clearly one typical example of his philanthropy which occurred after the war during a regular weekly visit to the Filey camp. He was apprehensively approached by the elderly secretary of a disabled organisation from Birmingham who wished to personally thank him for her marvellous holiday. She then politely enquired if it would be possible for the Guv'nor to donate a prize of two holidays so she could bring some more handicapped people to Butlin's.

Without hesitating the Guv'nor enquired: "How many members are you responsible for?"

" About 200," she replied.

Then turning to me he said: "Charles, go and give Clacton a ring and check on their bookings for September."

I left him signing autographs. He certainly was a celebrity in his own right. People constantly wanted to shake his hand and thank him for what in some cases was their first holiday experience.

When I returned to inform him that Clacton was only about half full on the dates in question he told me to take down the details of the lady's organisation and to block book all 200 of her members into the Clacton camp in late September free of charge. Needless to say the lady was astounded by his generosity.

After I had confirmed the booking with Clacton, the Guv'nor told me to telephone a national newspaper and give them the exclusive story about his goodwill gesture. That business flair was typical Bill Butlin. He may have had a heart of gold but he also never missed an opportunity for positive publicity. And that was another technique I also filed away for future reference.

Over the years I became a trusted member of Bill Butlin's personal staff, becoming to all intents and purposes his confidante and "Man Friday". I developed a close working and social relationship with the Guv'nor but after World War Two a change in his management policy led to me leaving the Butlin organisation.

I was the entertainments manager at Filey when the Guv'nor, responding to a post war government backed employment initiative, decided to offer senior managerial positions to high ranking military officers who had found it increasingly difficult to obtain work in civvy street since serving in the armed forces. In the press, much was again made of the Guv'nor's generosity, portraying him as a man of compassion. But it was felt, however, by the more objective thinking Butlin employees, that the practicality of those appointments left a great deal to be desired.

Dressed as a schoolmaster, centre, I'm ready with my band for another "Crazy Night" in the ballroom at Filey.

Standing room only as thousands of campers pack the Princess Ballroom at Filey to watch the band in "Arabian Nights".

Few, if any, of the new trainee managers had any background in the entertainment industry and they often made unilateral management decisions without consulting their more experienced staff. During one particular season at Filey the situation became increasingly unworkable and a cause of great personal frustration. For once I did not see eye to eye with the Guv'nor's innovation and I was left with no alternative but to tender my resignation.

When Bill Butlin received my official notification he was quite shocked at the depth of my feelings against what I considered to be blatant interference in the management and organisation of camp entertainment. As a result of my resignation I was invited to a meeting at the Filey entertainment office where the Guv'nor tried everything to persuade me to stay. However I was quite adamant about my position and I didn't change my mind. I simply could not work within the management structure as it then stood.

We eventually reached a fair compromise, the terms of which committed my dance band to regular summer seasons in the ballrooms at Filey and Skegness but released me to pursue my other diverse interests outside the Butlin organisation, on the understanding that if my expertise was ever required for camp development and alterations I would be available for immediate consultation.

The new arrangement , I am pleased to say, did not alter my personal relationship with Bill Butlin. We remained extremely close friends, so much so that when he eventually received his deserved knighthood in 1964 for services to the entertainment industry, my wife Margaret and I were among a select group of about 60 people who were invited to the celebrations in the Green Room of the Dorchester Hotel in London, where the guest of honour was Lord Louis Mountbatten.

CHAPTER THREE

Strike up the Band

With the outbreak of World War Two in 1939 the Butlin's site at Skegness was immediately closed to the public and requisitioned for personnel training by the Royal Navy, who renamed the camp HMS Royal Arthur. As a goodwill gesture all the campers affected by the closure received their money back, plus a coupon which promised them a free holiday once the hostilities had ceased. It was quite amazing how many of those people actually kept their coupons safe all through the war and returned to claim their free holiday when the camp reopened for the 1946 summer season.

After the closure of Skegness, I returned to Teesside and because of my artillery experience in the Territorial Army, I volunteered to be rear gunner in the Royal Air Force.

I passed all the written examinations and the initial local medical, but when I went to the Padgate airbase near Warrington for further training, the service's doctor took one look at my badly scarred right arm and sent me straight home on the first available train. So that rejection put an abrupt end to my personal war effort and fledgling military career.

Disappointed but hardly surprised, I found work as a night-time telephonist in Middlesbrough, then at ICI Billingham in the machine tool shop and finally in the Malleable Works drawing office in Stockton-on-Tees under the affable senior draughtsman, Johnny English.

Even in the early months of the hostilities it soon became apparent that Teesside was going to be a prime target for the hundreds of enemy aircraft who were endeavouring to paralyse the area's burgeoning industrial contribution to the British war effort.

The people of North Yorkshire and South Durham had to endure a constant stream of German bombing raids and although the local population coped well with the worry and uncertainty, every enemy sortie gradually undermined and eroded local morale.

In an effort to provide some light relief and entertainment in those hard times, I formed a dance band and we began organising our own local dances on Wednesday and Saturday nights. Our first performances were staged at the Queen's Hotel, near Middlesbrough station. In fact those functions proved to be so successful that we were eventually closed down and told our audiences were consuming the week's entire beer ration, which meant there was no liquid refreshment available for the regulars over the weekend.

That lame excuse wasn't wholly accurate because no sooner had our dances been terminated than the hotel management began to organise their own functions to cash in on our success. Their expansion plans were somewhat hindered, however, when a German bomb exploded near the railway station, wrecking the Queen's Hotel and, although I was sorry for the damage it caused, a small part of me smiled and said: "Poetic justice."

Undeterred and using my home as an office, I utilised the connections I'd made in the entertainment world at Skegness and continued to promote my own dances at a variety of hired venues in the North-east including the Baths Hall, Darlington, School Furnishing Headquarters, Darlington, and the Town Hall, Hartlepool. To ensure increased attendances at certain selected venues, I offered serviceman who brought a partner, free entry into the dance. That benevolent gesture virtually guaranteed me the house full signs and proved to be a sound public relations exercise on which to build.

The success of those promotions enabled me to utilise the vacant office space above another venue, the Palais de Danse in Stockton-on-Tees, and to buy what was then called the Mayfair Hall (later the Corporation Hall) which was also situated in Stockton.

Running parallel with the organisation of the dance promotions I was also hiring much larger theatres like the Middlesbrough Empire, the Stockton Empire and the Darlington Odeon in order to book the topline major stars of the day including Geraldo and his Orchestra, Gracie Fields, Larry Adler, Vic Oliver and Jimmy James. With tickets affordably priced at 2/6 and the house full signs again permanently up, business became very lucrative indeed.

My endeavours seemed to be filling a very convenient niche in the local entertainment market, which was based upon the public's insatiable desire for recreation as a much needed release valve from the worries of what was possibly the most difficult time in our country's modern history.

The Charles Amer Orchestra on stage at the Palais de Danse, Stockton-on-Tees, in March 1944.

*Over half a century later and I'm still presenting ballroom dancing every Saturday evening at the Marton Hotel.

Due to my success I was working full time as what can only be described as an impresario.

During the early days of the war I was constantly looking for competent musicians to fulfil my various engagements. I was endeavouring to run five bands, each with its own leader, and I regularly recruited new members from the County Durham area, particularly Ferryhill, Bishop Auckland and Spennymoor, which were hotbeds of brass band and musical talent.

It was at one of those auditions I met a very proficient double bass player called Eric Davison. He was a shift worker in the coal mines and we immediately struck up a good rapport together. He was an intelligent man, very likeable and a good communicator. Those were personal qualities which I admired and I soon realised I could utilise his talents to help with my flourishing entertainment business.

After some discussions with his employers, Eric was released from his essential job in the mines and joined me to initially promote my ENSA concerts. He later became my trusted right-hand man and band manager, organising all the bookings and travel arrangements to our nationwide venues. We worked together for almost 20 years and his conscientious assistance contributed greatly to the success the Charles Amer Orchestra eventually achieved. I wish to place on record how grateful I am for Eric's loyalty and hard work during the big band era.

Of all the many stars I promoted at that time I must single out Gracie Fields for a special mention. She was a lovely lady, a very down to earth performer with no edge or pretentions and although she was a famous name, she never acted like one. I remember one particular Sunday evening show just before she was due to go on stage, she noticed a young local singer in the wings suffering from a bad case of stage fright. Without hesitation she took the girl back to her dressing room and prepared a glass containing a mixture of port and brandy. That old pro's potion had the desired effect because as soon as the girl swallowed the liquid, it relaxed and lubricated her throat and settled her nerves. Once on stage the young lady sang like a bird and of course when Gracie performed she brought the house down.

There's an old adage which says good news always travels fast, and that observation certainly applied in my case during the early part of the war.

As a result of my success in staging local functions and events I was formally contacted in 1941 by the head of the Entertainments National Service Association and his deputy, the well known band leader Geraldo, and

Pictured at Filey with my trusty band manager of many years standing, Eric Davison.

invited to organise some concerts in the North-eastern area on their behalf. I was very flattered by their approach and accepted the task gladly.

ENSA was founded in August 1939 and had its headquarters at the Theatre Royal in Drury Lane, London. It was also fondly, but somewhat cruelly referred to as, Every Night Something Awful. That sarcastic jibe was the product of the rather amateurish standard of the concert acts it supplied, particularly at the beginning of the war, when the choice of available performing talent was at a premium.

The whole organisation was the brainchild of Basil Dean, an autocratic theatre producer and film magnate who had pioneered troop entertainment on a small scale through the Expeditionary Forces Canteen (EFC) during World War One. He was convinced servicemen would need morale boosting variety shows to help them cope with the stresses of war not only at home, but also aboard. He quickly obtained the assistance of the Navy, Army and Air Force Institutes (NAAFI) who provided the men and women of the services with canteens serving low cost food and with a place to meet and socialise.

The NAAFI also helped with the financing of the ENSA operation by ensuring every performing member received at least the princely sum of £10 a week. Although that appears to be a paltry amount now, it was in fact more than some of the artistes were earning at that time in regular theatre productions and was, for other performers, a much needed source of steady income.

Due to his forthright and brusque management style, Dean made many enemies, but he has to be applauded for his achievements because from very disorganised beginnings, ENSA flourished and its importance and influence grew. By the end of the war it was calculated that over three quarters of the British entertainment industry had at one time or another appeared under its banner. Stars like Vera Lynn, Gracie Fields, George Formby and Will Hay were some of the 4,000 performers who appeared in the 500 shows a week which Dean and his staff were promoting at home and overseas.

My own large local ENSA shows were usually held in midweek at either Thornaby Aerodrome, Goosepool near Middleton St. George or Catterick Camp in North Yorkshire. They all followed a similar presentation format, with two hours of band music, interspersed with vocal guest artistes. We often played to over 1,000 enthusiastic servicemen at a time and occasionally members of the audience, who were musicians in civvy street, joined us on stage to play, much to the enjoyment of their exuberant friends.

The largest concert my band ever attended took place at the Burtonwood American Airforce base near Warrington in Cheshire in one of their huge aircraft hangars. We must have played the Glenn Miller sound to nearly 5,000 raucous but very appreciative troops, surrounded by the imposing shapes of their large bombers.

It was while I was working for ENSA that Geraldo and myself were placed under temporary arrest after we took part in an unauthorised 15 minute pleasure flight over Teesside in a Flying Fortress from Thornaby Airfield. The American captain of the plane had been very impressed when during a conversation, Gerry told him that he actually knew Glenn Miller. So on the strength of that friendship we were given our exhilarating trip. When we touched down, however, we were all arrested by the airforce police and only released when the captain managed to convince the authorities he'd undertaken a legitimate training flight in order to carry out an important instrument check.

Years later I also found out from Lord Wigg, who became chairman of the Horseracing Betting Levy Board in the 1960s, that because I had access to so many of the country's air bases during the course of my ENSA work, the security services, and MI5 in particular, had investigated my activities and lifestyle in great detail. I must say I found the revelation a little unnerving to think that the authorities even contemplated a band leader could be involved in wartime espionage. Nevertheless, contained in some secret government filing cabinet there was a folder with the name Charles Amer on the front. Very John le Carré.

During that period I was dealing with scores of musicians and built up a professional reputation for being a firm but fair employer. Whatever the musicians' union rate was at any particular time I always endeavoured to pay more. I made sure the people I employed had few grounds for complaint and many stayed with me for years, so I take that recommendation to mean I must have been doing something right as a boss.

I learned very early on in my entertainment career, by observing the shrewd interpersonal skills of Bill Butlin, that a happy work force is one of the prerequisites for a successful and profitable business. That basic philosophy made an indelible impression on me. You must gain the respect, trust and confidence of your employees or they will feel no loyalty towards you or your company. Without those vital ingredients, you are only left with a recipe for potential failure.

Running concurrently with those large scale ENSA concerts, Bill Butlin was also promoting what he'd christened his reunion dances. Those events, which had started one New Year's Eve at Olympia, were part of a carefully devised strategy to enable the Guv'nor to keep in contact with his loyal patrons during the war years while his camps were closed and being used by military personnel. Those gatherings also continued for a short while after the war and sometimes proved so popular that the roads leading to the venues were often blocked solid with traffic.

In the early 1940s I was invited to provide the music for some of those reunion functions by Bill Butlin and although I had a touring band, raising the finance was a bit of a problem. But the Guv'nor told me not to worry about money because he would stand any losses on one condition, that I called the band Charles and his Butlin Boys. I had no objection to the concession and we toured around most of the major towns and cities in the country, where we were invariably packed to the rafters.

I remember one specific evening at Belle Vue in Manchester where we had an attendance of nearly 2,500 people, which was a house record at the time. In fact there used to be some good natured banter and rivalry between the various touring bands of that era like Joe Loss, Ivy Benson, Harry Roy, Ted Heath, Billy Ternant, Jack Payne, Henry Hall and Ken MacKintosh as to who could break the attendance records at particular venues and I pleased to say we were always up there with the best of them.

After about a year on the road I changed the name of the band back to Charles Amer and his Orchestra and we built up a very strong local and national following at venues as far afield as the Hammersmith Palais in London to Leeds, Cardiff and Glasgow. Apart from our live work, we also made some recordings of our numerous regular radio broadcasts on the popular BBC programme Workers' Playtime.

On reflection I am certain one of the main reasons for our longstanding popularity was that when we performed I always insisted we played in a strict dance tempo. I felt that conscious decision gave the orchestra its unique identity, which was much appreciated by our audiences and went some way to setting us apart from the crowd.

As a direct result of my work for ENSA I became firm friends with Geraldo and we attended many social and fund raising functions together both during and after the war. One particular evening in December 1944 we were invited to attend a cocktail party at the Savoy Hotel in London. It was held in honour of the great American band leader Glenn Miller who was on his way to Paris to do a radio broadcast for the allied troops. His band had gone on ahead and he intended to fly over to France to join them after the function. What a delightful evening we shared in Glenn Miller's relaxed and affable company.

Ivy Benson, pictured in her fur coat, and her famous all lady band, outside the Coatham Hotel in Redcar, with members of the Charles Amer Orchestra. Relationships became so friendly that there were five marriages between the musicians.

At the end of the proceedings Geraldo and myself were among the guests who walked down the steps of the Savoy and wished Glenn Miller goodnight as he boarded the military transport taking him to RAF Twinwoods, near Bedford, for the flight to France.

Of course we now know his plane mysteriously didn't reach Paris and despite numerous intensive searches of the proposed flight path the aircraft was never located. It was a dispiriting postscript to a marvellous personal experience. To lose a man who had contributed so much to the mass appeal of big band music in such strange and unexplained circumstances was very sad indeed. But at least I have the memory that I was one of the last people to see Glenn Miller alive and I still had the privilege of playing his timeless music to appreciative audiences.

During the early part of World War Two, as I have previously mentioned, the primary industrial area of Teesside was specifically targetted by waves of

German bombers who were endeavouring to disrupt and destroy the local factory output. The constant threat of those unexpected air-raids often made travelling to and from the local venues a very precarious business indeed.

I remember one booking at the Co-op Hall in Billingham when we were actually on stage playing for about 300 people and the warning sirens began. To avoid unnecessary panic we continued performing as the hall was evacuated by the police. But unlike the brave band members aboard the stricken liner Titanic we didn't wait around for the final scenario. As soon as it became apparent that a saturation bombing raid on the ICI was underway, and the hall was in grave danger of receiving a direct hit, we quickly made our way with all our instruments, with the exception of the drumkit and the piano, to the nearest shelter, where we stayed for about two hours before the all-clear was sounded.

But even then we had difficulty in returning to Middlesbrough because serious bomb damage had closed the road around the Cargo Fleet area and diversions were in operation. That particular evening developed into a very long night indeed and I eventually arrived home totally drained, at around 5am.

Another hairy incident occurred as we were travelling back to Teesside from a gig at the Baths Hall in Darlington. About 400 yards away from the road there was a blinding white flash as bombs exploded in the fields nearby. It was only when we saw the shells of the anti aircraft guns in the distance that we even realised there was an air-raid on RAF Goosepool at Middleton St. George in progress. Needless to say, I put my foot down and drove hell for leather out of the area as quickly as possible.

After another particularly heavy bombardment the entrance to the Farrer Street boxing arena in Middlesbrough was damaged, which resulted in the closure of the hall on safety grounds.

I was invited to examine the building by the part owner, Steve Buxton, and we established that fortunately there was no major structural damage and the repairs could be undertaken using only standard building materials.

I'm a very keen boxing fan and I felt it was important at that time to reopen the popular venue as quickly as possible. So in order to maintain the building as one of the much needed local amenities I bought a majority shareholding in the premises.

I applied for and obtained an official boxing promoter's licence and it was my intention to stage both professional boxing and wrestling at the arena. I also planned to utilise my Butlin connections and feature some of the more famous grappling names of the time, like Roughouse Baker and The Mask, to top the bill.

When the repairs to the arena were nearing completion I asked a popular local councillor, the very hardworking Tommy Meehan, if he would come and perform the re-opening ceremony, on the strict understanding that I would donate the whole of the first night's takings to any local charities of his choice. Acknowledging the gesture, he gladly accepted the invitation.

The wrestling was very well received indeed, with good attendances, but I had to eventually withdraw my support after a short time because I became aware that deliberate fight fixing (cheating by another name) was taking place and I wanted no part of it. That type of corrupt behaviour, where the results are predetermined by the participants or influenced by third parties, has no place in any sport. But at least I took some satisfaction from the fact that I'd ensured one of the popular local sporting facilities was again open to the general public.

Looking back at that period in my life from 1939-45 I've now come to realise that the music and entertainment I provided for both the troops and civilians was my own personal war effort. I was undoubtedly compensating for the physical injury which had denied me the opportunity to serve in the forces overseas. By becoming a band leader I found a worthwhile and rewarding substitute occupation which gave me the satisfaction that I was, even in a small way, "doing my bit" for King and Country during those troubled times.

Socialising with the famous band leader Joe Loss, left, and Mickey Marshall.

CHAPTER FOUR

And the band played on

During the early post war years The Charles Amer Orchestra became a popular resident attraction for the summer season at Butlin's Filey. On three separate occasions we also had the privilege of playing in front of 5,000 people at the Royal Albert Hall in London for the Guv'nor's reunion dances and at the Butlin sponsored National Ballroom Dancing Championships.

In August 1947 we made our debut on the silver screen in a period piece movie called Holiday Camp, which was directed by Ken Annakin.

The original story idea had been conceived by the popular radio personality Godfrey Winn and the screenplay was written by Muriel and Sidney Box, Ted Willis - who later wrote the long running police series Dixon of Dock Green - and Peter Rogers. The film starred Dame Flora Robson and Dennis Price as the well cast villain. It also introduced Jack Warner, Kathleen Harrison and Jimmy Handley as members of the famous, or infamous, depending on your taste, Hugget Family. The exploits of that working class family in Holiday Camp were to prove so successful that they eventually starred in a series of their own films in the early 1950s.

The distinguished actress Jean Kent was also in the original cast but had to withdraw because of flu, apparently aggravated by the inclement east coast weather.

The thin plot revolved around a murder mystery committed on the camp. More importantly, however, the movie also mirrored the social changes taking place in post war Great Britain after the landslide general election victory of Clement Attlee's Labour Party in 1945. The mood in the country was one of great optimism and the holiday camps had become the focus of the mass entertainment phenomenon, as people unashamedly enjoyed themselves after enduring six devastating and tragic years of war. Due entirely to Bill Butlin's imaginative business acumen, holiday camp entertainment had become synonymous with the major stars and celebrities of that period and it was a natural progression for the film industry to eventually capitalise on that notoriety, by using the location as a backdrop for an entire feature film.

In order to give the film an authentic setting, the film crews spent many weeks at Filey shooting the free activities which were provided for the campers.

As the resident band at Filey I was invited by Ken Annakin to play all the music for the ballroom sequences which were shot in the well-appointed and atmospheric Princess Ballroom. During the location shooting, some of our most popular Crazy Night comedy sketches, such as Little Nell and September in the Rain, were filmed and recorded to be edited into the appropriate scenes.

The interior filming was done at Gainsborough Studios and although we were required to be on the set for the purposes of continuity, we actually never played a note. It was all mimed and the soundtrack dubbed on later.

The band's constant miming during the studio filming led to a rather humorous incident, when one of the 400 extras in the ballroom scenes came up to me during a break in the shooting schedule and enquired: "Are you really musicians or just actors?"

"Why do you ask that?" I replied, somewhat puzzled by the question.

"Because we've never actually heard you play anything. All you do is mime."

She was right of course, because throughout the whole time it had taken to dub the ballroom scenes, no music had been played, so the actors' dialogue could be clearly recorded.

After my conversation with the extra I approached Ken Annakin and told him our credibilty as musicians was being called into question and would he mind if we played a few numbers just to prove we were in fact a "real band" and not just stand-ins, hired specifically to make up the cast list. Ken agreed to my request and we played a few of our favourite tunes for the "crowd". Our impromptu performance was greeted with rapturous enthusiasm by the gyrating masses, thus restoring our professsional esteem.

One scene I particularly remember from the film was when Ken Annakin

A scene from the successful Ken Annakin film "Holiday Camp". The Charles Amer Orchestra played all the music for the location sequences shot in the Princess Ballroom, Filey.

wanted a close up of a young girl performing a popular dance of the time called the Jitterbug. He turned to me and asked if there were any likely candidates for the role among the extras. I pointed out a pretty blonde girl who had been dancing with gusto and energy. After a brief audition she was duly selected to perform the dancing close-ups.

In those days as film extra you either had the option of being paid or having your name on the list of credits. The young dancer wisely chose the latter. She later became one of the most famous British film actresses of the 1950s - Diana Dors - and to think her film career all began dancing the Jitterbug to music provided by my band.

At Gainsborough Studios I had the privilege of meeting another talented actress of that period, Margaret Lockwood, albeit in rather unusual circumstances. She had been working on a stage nearby and during a break in her filming schedule she was attracted to the Holiday Camp set by the sound of my orchestra. At that time we were very close to completing our picture but I was having great difficulty dubbing some of my dialogue and it must have taken me over 30 attempts to finally synchronise it correctly.

After we eventually finished, much to Ken Annakin's and my relief, Margaret Lockwood came over to compliment me and the performance of the orchestra. She also told me not to worry about 'fluffing' my lines as she frequently did the same thing during filming and that I was still some way short of her record number of retakes, which was nearer 40. I must admit just knowing that even actresses of her distinction openly confessed to making mistakes helped alleviate my own sense of personal embarrassment.

During the 1950s we became good friends and when she had engagements in the North of England she often stayed with us at the Coatham Hotel. Unfortunately when I sold the Coatham in 1963 I left behind on the premises a personally signed picture which she had given me, an oversight which I now very much regret.

The completed movie turned out to be very successful indeed and a real major moneyspinner for the Rank Organisation. The Sunday Chronicle's review claimed: "It's true to life and will be a certain smash at the box office" and how right they were.

No doubt the size of the audiences was increased by the thousands of Filey holidaymakers who went along to their local cinemas to watch the movie in the hope of seeing themselves, however fleetingly, on the camp location shots.

The extent of my own personal movie career was dictated by the editing process because the duration of the ballroom scenes was unfortunately cut from the original cinema length of 40 minutes to an abridged television version of about eight. But at least I didn't totally end up on the cutting room floor and I thoroughly enjoyed the whole film making experience and remained firm friends with the film's director Ken Annakin.

Organising a touring band was often very hectic and time consuming. We spent many hours on the road and I am deeply indebted to my wife Margaret for all her support and understanding, as I endeavoured to establish a reputation in the entertainment world.

In the days before we could afford our own coach, the travel arrangements to the various venues were very basic indeed, comprising mainly of three or four cars crammed to the gunnels with sometimes as many as 16 musicians and instruments of all shapes and sizes. Breakdowns were frequent and on a few occasions I've even had to start a dance without a full band, because some of the lads were stranded on route.

I distinctly remember an incident when we were travelling to a Press Ball at Leeds City Hall and one of our three cars suddenly ground to an unhealthy halt. With no time for running repairs, we had to abandon the vehicle and pile as many bodies and instruments as we could into my Railton Special. How I managed to squeeze three in the front, five in the back, including one of my smallest musicians lying horizontally across the rear parcel shelf, and three in the boot I'll never know, but at least we arrived on time to fulfil the engagement.

Often, because of my business commitments on Teesside, I had to leave the band's travel arrangements in the capable hands of Eric Davison and I'd follow on later in my own car, hopefully arriving just before the gig started.

One particular wintery evening we were booked to perform at a Policemen's Ball in Oldham and some of the lads, because of the very poor weather conditions, set off early to make sure they'd arrive safely and in good time for the function.

Later in the afternoon when I eventually left Teesside for Lancashire in my Triumph Dolomite, the snow was falling heavily and the roads were being cleared by hard-pressed snowploughs. By the time I neared Leeds, the conditions were deteriorating rapidly, with freezing fog being the main driving hazard. It was obvious the weather was closing in, so I phoned Eric at the venue and informed him I was not going to make it and was returning to Middlesbrough.

During our conversation, however, he told me that one of the cars which was carrying some of our important equipment hadn't arrived and he'd received no confirmation as to its whereabouts. That unfortunate situation meant the resident band had to kindly lend some of our lads their instruments so we could play. As I returned to Teesside I kept a concerned and watchful eye open for my stranded musicians, but all to no avail.

The following morning Eric Davison and myself went around to Lenny Dawson's house to find out what had happened to them, only to be told nobody had seen him all night. That information made me very worried for their safety. So, armed with shovels, we drove back along their proposed route, looking for any vehicles which had been abandoned. But to our disappointment and growing unease, there was no sign of their car.

Then, quite by chance at the notorious Spa Hotel corner, on the A167 which runs between Northallerton to Darlington near Croft Aerodrome, we noticed a small plume of smoke slowly rising from the top of a large mound of snow piled high by the side of the road. Stopping to investigate, we began digging very carefully and uncovered, buried beneath the drift, the car which contained Lenny Dawson and his travelling companion. Fortunately they were quite safe and sound.

Apparently they'd skidded off the main road and slammed into the roadside drift with such force that the weight of snow had cacooned them in their vehicle overnight, hidden from view. Luckily they had some sandwiches with them but because the car doors couldn't be forced open they'd had to stay put and hope to be located the following day. When I eventually managed to release them Lenny said, as calm as you like: "Hello boss, I was wondering when somebody was going to find us."

To recount the story now, it all sounds very amusing, but at the time it was quite possible if we hadn't found them when we did, they could have quite easily died of hypothermia because the weather had shown no obvious signs of abating. They were, I'm glad to say, none the worse for their overnight ordeal.

Constant touring with the band was physically very demanding but it also had its lighthearted compensations and humorous incidents, as you would come to expect when a large group of men were continually on the road together.

I remember one Friday evening in the early Fifties, we'd been playing one of our many popular gigs at the Beverley Road Baths in Hull for the local Fish Friers Association, when on our journey home a swarthy young man suddenly darted out of the roadside undergrowth into the middle of the A19.

He then proceeded to frantically wave a very large piece of white material in the beam of the headlights, as if he wished to surrender.

As we carefully pulled up alongside him, I wound down the window and noticed the white material was in fact part of a parachute. As I enquired if we could be of any assistance he breathlessly explained, in broken English, he was a Saudi Arabian trainee pilot who'd bailed out of his aircraft due to technical difficulties and asked if we could give him a lift. He was rather confused and in a state of shock so we decided the best plan of action was to take him to York police station.

We recounted the evening's events to the rather sceptical desk sergeant and were only allowed to continue on our journey home after the pilot had confirmed our version of the story.

The following morning Margaret woke me up by saying there was a newspaper reporter at the front door wanting an exclusive interview about the aircraft pilot I'd given a lift to the previous evening. Apparently I was being proclaimed as some sort of hero because, unbeknown to me, the pilot was in fact a Saudi Arabian Prince.

I didn't bother talking to the reporter because as far as I was concerned it was a charitable act and one for which I was not seeking any publicity. But later in the day when I drove into Middlesbrough the early evening papers were proclaiming from their numerous billboards dotted around the town: "Local dance band leader rescues royal foreign airman."

It only serves to emphasise how the most innocuous of events can be interpreted in order to produce prominent headline copy.

A short while later I surprisingly received an official communique from the Saudi Arabian Embassy in London conveying their profoundest thanks for my efforts, which was all very gratifying but rather embarrassing, as all I'd done was to play the role of the Good Samaritan and taken a confused and distressed young man to the nearest police station where he could receive some assistance.

There were many changes of personnel in the band over the years and we often had to audition musicians while we were on the road. I vividly remember the events of a particular evening when we were playing the King's Hall, Bradford, in the early 1950s. We'd advertised in the local press for a trumpeter and eight prospective candidates arrived at the venue. As they were auditioning, it very quickly became apparent that one player was technically outstanding, and far superior to the others in both his style and the quality of sound. I did, however, have grave reservations about him because my professional intuition told me he was too much of an individualist to gel within the structure of a band. I discussed my doubts with Eric Davison and we politely turned him down for the position.

At that time I had no idea who he was, but he did look rather shocked when I explained my reasons for not offering him the job.

Before long my appraisal of his talent was to be proved very accurate indeed. His name was Eddie Calvert and he was later christened "The Man With The Golden Trumpet". He went on to become a world famous soloist and recording star, with such instrumental hit records in 1954/55 as Oh Mein Papa and Cherry Pink and Apple Blossom. I certainly know a good musician when I see one and who knows, my honest professional assessment may have provided the vital catalyst which ignited his solo career.

Contrary to popular opinion the music business is not a glamorous life. The condition of some of the crumbling venues we performed in left a lot to be desired and occasionally the changing facilities and digs we encountered were at best, unhygienic. But even through all the trials and tribulations we had a marvellous time and no matter where we were playing or how late I had retired to bed the previous evening, I was always up at 8:30 the next morning ready for work.

In the early 1950s I began an annual festive ritual which has continued to this day. It originated when, without our knowledge, a Humberside promoter advertised that my band would be performing at a New Year's Eve Ball to reopen the New City Hall in Hull which had suffered extensive bomb damage during the war.

Normally during the Christmas period I restricted myself to traditional local engagements, including the Redcar Rugby Club dance at the Coatham, so I could be at home to enjoy the Yuletide celebrations with my family. In an effort to decline the Hull engagement we requested three times our normal fee, thinking the greatly increased demand was bound to be unacceptable and therefore lose us the booking.

However to our total surprise, the promoter replied we were the only band he wanted and he'd already been selling tickets on the strength of our appearance, even though he'd given us no official notification of the booking. The fee he told us was also acceptable, because being the New Year any extra financial outlay would be covered by the higher ticket prices he was charging.

The protracted contract negotiations took an even more bizarre twist when on one occasion the promoter, who was obviously beginning to fret at the possibility of our non-appearance, failed to make urgent contact with Eric Davison. In his blind panic he phoned the local Redcar constabulary who arrived at the Coatham Hotel where Eric was living, only to find him contentedly soaking in the bath wondering what all the fuss was about.

When one of the Coatham Hotel's directors, the respected Redcar councillor Alf Wright, discovered the band would not be playing on Teesside for the New Year, he came to see me with an unusual request.

One Hogmany, Alf had presented me with a gold sovereign in the hope that the luck he said I possessed would be transferred to him. Even though he knew I would be performing in Hull, he was quite insistent I gripped the coin very tightly at midnight to ensure continued good fortune. Not wishing to disappoint him I promised to do as he asked.

The dance at Hull was a rather grand affair with the gentlemen wearing dinner jackets and the ladies resplendent in their long gowns and finery. Close on midnight the band were ready to strike up Auld Lang Syne when my lead sax player saw me taking the gold sovereign out of my pocket and asked what it was. Playing along with Alf Wright's superstition I explained if you touched the coin at midnight it would bring you a great deal of luck for the forthcoming year. No sooner had I finished the implausible explanation than the message spread like wildfire through the members of the band and they all reached over to receive the mystical power of the gold sovereign.

The ballroom's master of ceremonies, who had noticed the commotion on stage among the musicians, came over to enquire if there was a problem. I then had to explain to him they were all trying to touch my lucky gold coin.

As I was repeating the story of the sovereign's significance to him, the hall's public address system was still switched on, so my voice was being broadcast through his MC's microphone to the entire audience, who by now had stopped to listen attentively to my explanation.

Then, after we had played in the New Year, literally hundreds of the revellers queued up to touch the lucky gold coin.

The following Saturday we were playing our regular date at the Coatham Hotel's Windsor ballroom when to my surprise a lady informed me she'd been told about the special properties of a lucky gold sovereign which I apparently possessed. Quite how the story had travelled from Hull to Redcar so quickly I can only speculate, but in no time at all, scores of people were once again queueing to touch the coin.

Alf Wright didn't know what he'd started when he presented me with the sovereign. And from that day to this, the New Year coin touching ritual has become permanently etched into my life. Over the last 45 years thousands of people must have participated in the charade. Even today I'm still approached on a New Year's Eve so superstitious people can touch the keepsake for luck.

With regard to my own fortune, I've often been asked whether or not I believe in the sovereign's power and my answer is always the same, the coin never leaves my pocket.

Another example of a personal habit which later became a superstition involved my own entrance onto the stage which was always from the right of the platform as the band played our familiar signature tune, Small Hotel. I am not sure where, when or why I started the routine, but during our many years of performing I never broke the tradition, just in case it affected our success. And I'm glad to say it never did.

The Charles Amer Orchestra always played in a wide variety of towns and cities all over the country even in venues which had dubious reputations, like Green's in Glasgow and the dance halls of Cardiff's Tiger Bay area. We encountered very little trouble because we were acknowledged within the profession as an accomplished orchestra who played the type of dance music the people wanted to hear. I also made a concerted effort to cultivate a good line in repartee with the audience by utilising the communication skills I'd learned at Butlin's. That technique ensured there was always a good natured atmosphere at our gigs.

Apart from performing on Teesside - which strangely enough many visiting bands also regarded as a tough area - my favourite towns in which to play were Leicester, Nottingham, Belle Vue Manchester, and the Beverley Road Baths in Hull. Just like footballers who have particular preferences for certain soccer grounds I enjoyed playing at certain venues. In hindsight it was possibly something to do with an auditorium's acoustics and how the band's sound was projected which affected my choice.

While researching material for this publication, and reminiscing through my old photograph albums and press cuttings, I have reaffirmed what I believed 45 years ago that Teesside was one of the premier areas in the country for dance band music.

Listed below is a randomly chosen weekend in February 1952 when the public could chose from over a dozen different venues, each with a band performing live music.

I wonder how many of these once thriving dance halls and musicians evoke fond memories of readers' formative years out on the town:

CHARLES AMER & HIS FAMOUS ORCHESTRA

PLAY FOR DANCING EVERY WEDNESDAY & SATURDAY AT THE

COATHAM HOTEL REDCAR

15 star musicians
With featured B.B.C. Vocalist
Carole Scott

Under the personal supervision of the Smiling Maestro of the Screen,
CHARLES AMER

WATCH THIS COLUMN FOR NEW FEATURES WEEKLY WITH GUEST ARTISTES AND EVENTS OF INTEREST.

Tel. 83.   Tel. 83.

A rather flattering publicity photograph of myself, resplendent in full evening attire taken around 1947.

AEU Hall - Jimmie Burns and his Orchestra; Maison de Danse Stockton - Jack Marwood and his Orchestra; Palais de Danse Stockton - Bob Potter and his Claviolins; Jubiliee Ballroom Stockton - Cecil Jack and his Orchestra; RAF Club Thornaby - Bob Nelson and his Blue Rhythm Orchestra, plus Billy Jackson and his band; Billingham Co-op Hall - Billy Riche and his Orchestra; Norton Co-op Hall - Len Madden with his Xylophone and Orchestra; Carlton Ballroom - Hilda Stephens; Pier Ballroom Redcar - Danny Mitchell and his Hawaiians featuring Kaluha and Tony James; Swan Hotel Redcar - Harry Thorpe and his Orchestra; Town Hall Middlesbrough - Jimmy Carr and his Orchestra plus the Carrisma players; Linthorpe Assembly Rooms - Joe Hurst and his Orchestra; St Alphonus Hall - Ernie Wilson and his band; Empress Ballroom Middlesbrough - Bert Waller and his Orchestra.

What a fine selection of predominantly local musicians and vocalists are contained in the listing, many of whom I knew personally and held in high regard, particularly Jack Marwood, pianist Billy Daniels and saxophonist Marsha Newton.

During the course of my successful professional career I dread to think how many hundreds of thousands of miles I've travelled with the band and on business. I've also been very fortunate to purchase vehicles of real quality in which to make those journeys. If I had to chose any particular favourite make of car it would certainly have to be a Rolls Royce because of their reliability, style and craftsmanship. They are one of the few cars which actually appreciates in value once they've been purchased.

I remember with great amusement an episode which revolved around an order I placed over the telephone relating to the purchase of a new car.

Before taking delivery of a Rolls Royce you are given the opportunity to customise the car to suit your own taste, even down to choosing the original livery. So when I conveyed all my personal specifications to one of Rolls' main dealerships, Jack Barclay's of London, they enquired about my choice of colour. I replied that I wanted the car to be a shade darker than British racing green.

A short while later the paint shop manager at the company's production headquarters in Crewe phoned to confirm my choice of colour because apparently it was a rather unique shade, even for Rolls Royce. I then reiterated my request about my preference for a touch more green.

When I eventually received a call from Barclay's informing me the car was ready for collection, Margaret and my son Kevan were coincidently in London on business. I therefore suggested to Kevan it would be more convenient if he collected the new Rolls and drove it back to Teesside.

Later the same day I phoned their hotel to see if the collection had gone smoothly and Kevan told me the car's original colouring had attracted numerous admirers, some of whom had taken photographs while it was parked outside the hotel.

At the end of the same week I was at Normanby Hall when the dogs, sensing one of the family was returning home, began to bark, so I automatically looked out of the window to see who was coming up the drive. Well! I couldn't believe my eyes when I saw Kevan behind the wheel of a pale green almost mustard coloured Rolls Royce. My initial reaction when I saw the car for the first time was to say to myself: "My God, I can't drive that!"

I hastily rang the paint shop in Crewe and asked what was the name of the colour. To my surprise they said it didn't have a registered trade name because, being so highly unique, it was still only known as colour code 88.

Enquiring further as to how the new car's colour could differ so widely from my original choice, it transpired the paint shop manager had misheard my telephone instructions. Instead of carrying out the request of add more green, it had been interpreted as add more CREAM, hence the drastic colour change.

I phoned Jack Barclay's to canvass their opinion about the colour and a company representative said they thought I'd gone mad when they took delivery of the car from Crewe. But surprisingly he said, as it stood in the showroom waiting for Kevan to collect it, many enquires about how to order a car of a similar colour were received. Eventually the colour was named Amazon Green and added to the Rolls stock list. It also later appeared on other makes of car like the Jaguar.

My family became quite attached to the unique looking car and I must say after the initial shock, so did I. We used it as the main car at Kevan's wedding and it never lost its public attraction. No matter where the Rolls was parked it was always guaranteed to be admired. When I eventually sold the car some years later, I received four times the original purchase price. I suspect that was due in part to the unique colour which had resulted from a simple misunderstanding with the paint shop at Crewe thinking I said cream, instead of green.

Margaret takes a front seat in the infamous cream-green Rolls Royce.

CHAPTER FIVE

Variety is the spice of life

Just after World War Two I became very involved with the Variety Club of Great Britain's fund raising activities. My mentor Bill Butlin had introduced me to the organisation as a barker and I later became Chief Barker of the Teesside area, before it merged with Newcastle to form the North-eastern region.

This very worthy, worldwide voluntary organisation whose primary objective is to help sick, disabled and disadvantaged children was established in America in 1928. It evolved out of the compassionate actions of a group of showbusiness people who came together to help a baby which had been abandoned at the Sheridan Theatre in Pittsburgh. Their first organised event was staged in a big top, so all the terminology appertaining to the Variety Club is derived from the world of the circus. Each club is called a tent, with Pittsburgh being No.1 and the Variety Club of Great Britain, which was created in 1949, No.36.

Members of the club are called barkers, a term attributed to the raucous individuals who were employed to shout: "Roll up, roll up", outside the circus tent in an effort to encourage potential customers to sample the delights of the attractions inside. The title of Chief Barker is given to the president of a particular tent.

Since its formation nearly 50 years ago, the Variety Club of Great Britain has raised over £100 million for the underprivileged children of this country and is supported in its work by nine regional committees including the North-east.

Over the years many of the stars of cinema, television and business have given their time, free of charge, at award ceremonies, lunches, film premiers and sporting events in order to further the aims and objectives of the Variety Club. As a result of their generosity the running and administration costs of the organisation are very low indeed. For every pound donated, 90 pence goes to the youngsters who need it most. This must be one of the highest donation percentages attained by any charity and is a credit to the members.

Being a member of the Variety Club has given me an immense amount of personal satisfaction and has enabled me to meet people of influence and stature, including her majesty the Queen and Prince Philip. I'm proud to repeat that I'm a staunch royalist and believe most passionately in the monarchy and the good it does our country. The institution is highly respected aboard and I have nothing but admiration for the way the Queen has conducted herself in recent years while the tabloid press has taken great delight in exposing the human frailties of her family. I have been fortunate enough to be invited to Buckingham Palace several times on Variety Club business and have found her Majesty and Prince Philip to be very well informed and keenly interested with regard to the organisation's work.

One of the most embarrassing incidents of my whole life involved the Queen when she came to Teesside on an official visit during her Jubilee tour of the nation. My wife and I were among numerous local people invited aboard the royal yacht Britannia for an informal cocktail party.

We queued on the quayside to be introduced to Her Majesty but when it was our turn to shake hands with the Queen I became totally overwhelmed by the experience, and for the one and only time in my public life I was not in control of my actions. I have no recollection to this day of what she said to me or even if I replied coherently. The moment just simply passed me by. I was in awe of being in her majesty's presence. On reflection it was a rather humbling experience.

For over 15 years during the 1960s and 70s my wife Margaret and her hard working committee organised many garden parties on behalf of the Variety Club in the grounds of my home, Normanby Hall, which were attended by thousands of local people.

Those informal fund-raising events, which became a permanent fixture on the summer social calendar, always took place on Sunday afternoons in June and often featured stalls, sideshows, competitions, games and displays by police horses. All the food was prepared by the chefs at our hotels and was then brought to Normanby Hall in time for the festivities.

Crowds of over 5,000 attended the many Variety Club open days staged in the grounds of my home, Normanby Hall.

Margaret presents the trophy to the winning jockey of one of the races we sponsored at Stockton racecourse.

Prior to the inaugural event I lightheartedly decreed the opening day would be warm and sunny, and surprisingly it was. From then on all the other functions were blessed with fine weather. I don't think I possess any mystical power which controls the elements, but we never had to cancel a single occasion due to inclement weather, which taking into account the unpredictability of the British climate was some achievement.

After I'd fully developed the Marton Hotel site in Middlesbrough during the 1960s I also organised numerous dinner dances and functions on behalf of the Variety Club which again helped to raise many thousands of pounds for deprived children. I was particularly proud when our North-eastern regional committee was one of the first in the country to deliver (sorry, no pun intended) a fully equipped purpose built ambulance to assist with the transfer of pregnant women to hospital.

One of the most popular charity events I organised took place in 1971 when we needed 400 men to drink 3,000 pints of free beer generously donated by local breweries. Surprisingly we had little difficulty in finding the required number of participants for the tasting festival which not only helped to raise glasses, but also funds, for the Variety Club.

Over the years I've also had formal and informal links with many organisations which work tirelessly away from the glare of publicity to provide comfort for others, including the Dunkirk Veterans Association and the Rotary Organisation. I have, however, made a conscious decision not to dwell on my personal involvement with regard to sponsorship or fund raising for charity, except to say if everybody was more sympathetic to the needs of others, then the world would be a far better place.

Today as I write I fear as a nation we're becoming too selfish and losing our compassion and tolerance for our fellow citizens at both home and aboard. As the developed world constantly strives through technological advances for greater material wealth, people are becoming more self-centred and as a consequence the family relationships which should be the bedrock of society seems to be suffering. Surely in the long term that cannot be good for the future social stability of this or future generations.

It is my belief these negative personal attitudes will only perpetuate an erosion of society 's moral values if they are not tackled at the highest level soon. Possibly the first new of government for nearly 20 years (May 1997) might herald that much needed change.

In the 1970s my wife and I were members of a British delegation invited to participate in the tenth anniversary celebrations of the Israeli Variety Club.

During our visit we attended the foundation stone laying ceremony for a disadvantaged children's hospital that the Variety Club of Great Britain were helping to fund. When it was completed the new four storey building contained all the modern medical facilities. Eric Morley, the chairman of the Mecca entertainments group which promoted the Miss World contest, was a member of the party and he may well have been the Chief Barker of the Variety Club at the time.

Margaret and I had a marvellous week visiting all the places of biblical significance like the Dead Sea, Galilee and Bethlehem. We were particularly impressed by the city of Jerusalem where we were introduced to the mayor, Teddy Gardiner, who had once lived in England. We also met Israeli president, Ephraim Katzir, and had dinner with the prime minister, Menachem Begin, who was a very pleasant man indeed. It was hard to imagine in his younger days he had been a ruthless freedom fighter.

One famous member of the tour party, who doubled both as our host and guide for the whole trip, was the renowned Israeli actor and singer Topol who came to worldwide prominence for his leading role in the popular stage and film musical, Fiddler on the Roof. What a genial character he was, full of life and very enthusiastic about showing us the rich culture of his country. His effervescent personality certainly contributed a great deal to make our stay enjoyable.

Many of the people we met on our visit were very welcoming and the reception we received was excellent. We saw no hint of unrest in an area which only a few years previously had been at war with its neighbours.

On one particular excursion to the Wailing Wall and the extensive caves nearby, we were escorted by a very amiable and informative young rabbi. I was so impressed by his competency that I asked Topol what would be an appropriate tip to give him. The amount suggested was a hundred. So at the end of the visit I approached the rabbi to say how much I'd enjoyed the day and gave him the token of my appreciation. When he saw the money he was astonished and gestured as if to refuse the gift, until I insisted he accepted.

As we were leaving on the coach Topol, who must have noticed the surprised expression on the face of the rabbi, asked me if I'd had a pleasant day. I replied it had been most enjoyable but when I told him I'd given the guide a £100 tip, he gasped in amazement and said: "A hundred pounds, surely you mean a hundred sheckels?"

"No a hundred pounds," I confirmed.

Apparently I'd paid nearly five times as much as he'd originally suggested. My gift should have been in the Israeli currency of sheckels but I'd misunderstood and given my gratuity in pounds. No wonder the young rabbi was delighted. Come to think of it at the time I thought it was a little excessive, but it was worth it for such an excellent trip.

Although the Variety Club has many committed members, in modern times there has been a tendency for petty jealousies to surface, particularly when the honours lists are published.

I feel very strongly that charitable work should be freely undertaken to help those who are in need and not be used or even abused as a blatant public relations exercise to enable fading personalities to stay in the limelight.

Keeping a low profile, however, has not always been adopted by the contemporary so called stars, whose manipulative advisers decide whether attendance at a specific event will promote a positive or negative image of their client. From my point of view the motive for participation is morally important, and while some charities do undoubtedly benefit particularly from royal patronage, I am generally very sceptical about the involvement of celebrities in charity work.

Margaret and I meet president Ephraim Katzir during our visit to celebrate the tenth anniversary of the Israeli Variety Club.

Some of the hard working members of the Variety Club outside the Marton Hotel with a Sunshine Coach bought with funds raised by the Teesside branch. Left to right, Dick Smith, Jack Doberman, Ronnie Goodman, Stan Thompson, Harry Simon and Charles Amer.

If in the past I had maximised the potential of every event I attended or every possible photo opportunity, I would never have been out of the papers or the gossip columns. No, my criteria for supporting a worthy cause has always been either to make a donation anonymously or with the minimum amount of fuss. If you need the publicity then you are involved for the wrong reasons.

Another organisation which has given me a great deal of pleasure through the years is the National Sporting Club. Once again I have Bill Butlin to thank for introducing me to that prestigious boxing organisation which from 1955 to 1983 was based at the salubrious Cafe Royal in London's Piccadilly.

The National Sporting Club can trace its roots directly back to the boisterous days of the 18th Century and the outlawed, but very popular, bareknuckle fighting era. It grew from the need to regulate that underground sport and it is generally recognised as the first body to enforce the rules of boxing, as laid down by the Marquis of Queensberry.

By the beginning of the 20th Century the NSC was established as a traditional gentleman's club in Covent Garden and was awarding the much coveted Lonsdale Belts, named after its first president, the Earl of Lonsdale. When boxing became a fully accepted and recognised international sport, the control and overall organisation was eventually passed into the hands of the British Boxing Board of Control, the Amateur Boxing Association and the Olympic Committee. The NSC became purely a social organisation. After leaving the original premises in 1929 the Club had several homes before it came to rest in 1955 at the Cafe Royal with Charles Forte as its president.

In more recent times the main function of the Club has been to promote the positive aspects of boxing and provide entertainment for its members, while at the same time enabling young fighters to demonstrate their boxing prowess in public. Those traditional and formal monthly events gave an opportunity to many young men to box before a quiet, knowledgeable and appreciative audience of boxing conniosseurs. After about ten years I was accorded the honour of being made an honourary vice president and because of my connections in the entertainment world I was often involved in the organisation of the famous celebrity dinners, when notable sportsmen like Jack and Bobby Charlton and Henry Cooper would be the guests of honour.

Members of the Teesside Variety Club present Margaret and I with a silver salver to commemorate our fund raising activities.

One of the most outstanding nights in the distinguished history of the National Sporting Club occurred in 1960, when a banquet for over 360 guests was held in honour of past and present boxing champions. The guest of honour was Frenchman Georges Carpentier, the famous world light-heavyweight champion of the 1920s along with Kid Berg, Len Harvey, Ted Lewis, Freddie Mills, Bombardier Billy Wells and Jimmy Wilde. I was fortunate enough to be seated at one of the top tables for such a marvellous evening of memories and nostalgia.

My love of boxing has already been noted and I was rather sad to hear of the NSC's demise when under the guise of the Anglo/American Boxing Club it moved to the Grosvenor Hotel because I really enjoyed the ambiance of those social evenings. It has, however, I am pleased to see, been revived by former England test cricketer Bob Willis's corporate promotions company and is once again based along with its original title at the Cafe Royal.

Although as a former council member of the original club I have received many formal invitations to attend their now more diverse sporting functions, I have not yet done so because of the furore surrounding the unfounded and embarrassing libellous allegations made against me in the 1980s which meant I consciously curtailed my social visits to London.

The council of the National Sporting Club contained some of the country's most eminent men.

CHAPTER SIX

Renovation And Construction

My interest in the building trade evolved steadily over a period of 60 years beginning in the late 1920s when I learnt some rudimentary drawing skills in the design office of Dorman Long's Lackenby Steelworks near Middlesbrough.

One of the chief design engineers in that office was George Gowland who worked on the specifications for the famous Sydney Harbour Bridge in Australia. George was a first class teacher and was a man I trusted implicitly. We eventually became firm friends when he gave me sound advice on matters relating to the building and engineering projects I undertook on behalf of Middlesbrough Football Club during my time as a director and chairman.

When I subsequently went to work for Bill Butlin, first at Skegness and later at Filey, it was a time of great opportunity in the entertainment business and I became deeply involved with the design and development of the camps' ballrooms and restaurants. Those facilities were constantly being expanded and upgraded to cater for the ever changing needs of the thousands of holidaymakers who were by then flocking to Butlin's.

That design input, which was right at the heart of the burgeoning Butlin empire, quickly increased my knowledge of the processes conducive to the construction industry, such as the use of various cost effective materials and the organisation of labour.

I also gained some relevant early practical experience during the 1939 summer season at Skegness when we had a fire in one of the large camp restaurants. After surveying the damage, Bill Butlin, ever the taskmaster, wanted the charred and gutted facility reopened within a fortnight. That restrictive time scale was very demanding but with the good organisation of men and resources, we accomplished the refurbishment in 18 days, much to the Guv'nor's satisfaction.

When therefore in 1945 I began renovating the Coatham Hotel in Redcar and some of the local Teesside dance venues such as the Palais de Danse and Corporation Hall in Stockton-on-Tees, I knew exactly how, and to what standards, I wanted to build my own developments.

Apart from working in Dorman Long's drawing office for a short time, all my building skills have been acquired through practical experience. That has meant spending many long hours on detailed planning and design work before the first foundations of any projects were even laid.

In the early days I accumulated my building knowledge by logically and carefully solving any on-site problems as they arose. For example in the 1960s, when I bought the old South Bank Empire cinema and obtained planning permission to turn it into a night club, in order to create more space, I had to replace the vertical pillars separating the stalls and the circle with a horizontal steel beam support. I put the work out to tender but the quotes I received from other firms were far too expensive, so I decided to undertake the conversion work myself.

The beam, which was 62 feet long and weighed four tonnes, stopped the traffic when it was delivered and drew a large crowd of bystanders to watch it being rolled into the building, through the emergency fire exit, on the three inch metal pipes. Once inside it was carefully manoeuvred on to three heavy duty lorry jacks which I'd hired. Then, without using a crane and utilising the diligent assistance of eight men over two days, we painstakingly managed to elevate the beam into the required position, by systematically underpinning it with a large number of nine by three inch wooden timbers.

The successful completion of the delicate operation certainly surprised the engineers from South Durham Steel who came to inspect the installation, because they had initially intimated it couldn't be done using my simple but practical method. But that's typical of my reaction to problem solving, I just enjoy proving the sceptics wrong.

Some 40 years ago, planning applications were less complicated than they are today. The officers in the local planning departments adopted a much more commonsense approach to new applications and they were often very positive in their comments, even going so far as to suggest the relevant amendments needed before re-application.

For example, when I added the new wing to the Coatham Hotel I was advised what type of lime bricks would conform to the planning requirements in order to complement the building's facade, and where to locate them.

Over the years, however, that helpful atmosphere seems to have been gradually eroded and become more confrontational and at times downright obstructive. Today applications often become increasingly enmeshed in constricting red tape and bureaucracy which I'm sure only serves to inhibit new building initiatives.

I've always endeavoured to retain personal control over my own building work, right from the initial design stage, through to the on-site supervision. My management style has always been very much a "hands on" approach to construction, the theory being if anything went wrong I only had myself to blame.

Financially I've tried to never overstretch my operations, by adopting the policy of only building to order. My company Parkway Estates also employed a manageable workforce of between 30 and 40 people, many of whom stayed loyal to me for many years, which again must say something positive about my staff management technique.

However unfortunate and unforseen financial circumstances - which will be fully explained in a later chapter - resulting from the "knock on" effect of possible litigation between myself and Middlesbrough Football Club in the 1980s meant I had to scale down, but not as was wrongly reported in some misinformed quarters liquidate, Parkway's operations. The consequences of that decision meant the enforced redundancy of many of my loyal local workforce including my trusted building foreman of 30 years standing, Bill Carvell.

On Tuesday, March 16, 1948, I attended an auction at the Wellington Hotel on Albert Road, Middlesbrough, with the intention of purchasing a tract of land to the South-east of the town which included Normanby Hall.

I had never been to an auction before and unfortunately my inexperience with regard to the speed of the bidding process meant I was unsuccessful in acquiring the lot I desired. At the end of the proceedings, however, I approached the buyer, CJ Jackson, who was a butcher from Darlington, and offered him what I thought was a very realistic price for the hall, its three cottages, the lodge, five outbuildings, two walled gardens and surrounding 74 acres. He must have also thought the price was reasonable because without much deliberation he accepted my offer and I signed a cheque for the appropriate amount there and then to conclude the purchase.

The picturesque Normanby Hall had fallen into a state of disrepair before I began its renovation in 1948.

It was rather ironic that I should have bought the Normanby Hall estate because as a youngster my friends and I, particularly in the school holidays, used to raid the large orchards in the grounds and we were forever being chased away by the gardener cum caretaker who diligently patrolled the premises. It was a great cat and mouse game played without malice which we enjoyed.

From the outset my overall plan and longterm intention was to totally demolish the neglected hall and build my own luxury bungalow on the same site.

However, after legal enquiries, that idea was scuppered when we were officially notified that the hall, which had been built in the early 19th Century, was in fact a Grade Two listed building and therefore protected, making restoration rather than demolition the priority.

In hindsight it would have been sacrilege to raze the hall to the ground because, even though it was in very poor condition, it was still an extremely impressive building comprising of 42 rooms which included five reception rooms, a library, billiard room, 15 bedrooms, two Adam style fireplaces and an Adam style ceiling.

The previous owners of the hall were a famous North-eastern family called the Ward Jacksons, who had owned the land since 1764 and had played a significant part in the embryonic industrial and social development of West Hartlepool during the Victorian era.

Some of the family had been people of great influence and were Members of Parliament, others clergy, but at the time of my acquisition of the property in 1948, the hall was uninhabited and on lease to Dickson and Benson of Linthorpe Road, Middlesbrough, as a furniture repository and storage space for pianos.

A short while after I'd acquired the hall I heard through the grapevine it was still officially classified as an unoccupied building on the council property register. Due to that classification it appeared on a list of possible sites to be developed into an old people's residential home. A local authority inspection, to gauge its suitability for that purpose, was imminent.

At that time my family and I were living in a pleasant bungalow on Ormesby Road, Middlesbrough. It was a property we had rented quite by chance having only seen it as we passed by in a removal van on our way to rent another house. I immediately stopped the van to inspect the bungalow and was so impressed with what I saw that I literally rented it on the spot.

To avoid any attempt to serve a compulsory purchase order on Normanby Hall I had to prove I was in fact living there, even though it was in a state of disrepair. My first move was to pay the rates, which gave the property a legal residential status. Secondly I placed some furniture in one of the few inhabitable rooms of the hall to at least give the impression I was now a permanent occupant.

When the inspection day arrived, three large black limousines carrying the po-faced local Middlesbrough councillors came up the drive in convoy and parked in front of what they no doubt thought was a derelict building.

As I walked around to the front entrance to "greet" them, I could hear their positive initial reactions and various favourable references to its great potential for development.

When I asked if I may be of any assistance, the astounded look on the face of the town clerk, who was just about to nail a notice to the front door, was a picture.

"Mr Amer, what are you doing here?" he enquired, in a rather startled tone.

" I live here," I confidently replied and added: " Please don't put any nail marks on my front door as it spoils the timber and then I'll be forced to sue you."

My request to safeguard the condition of the front entrance was rather hilarious because any further marks on the already flaked, scratched and weathered surface would have been extremely difficult to detect.

I gladly produced the rates receipt when my ownership of the property was questioned by the town clerk and as the farrago continued I could see in the background a good friend of mine, Councillor Tommy Meenan, trying unsuccessfully to subdue a smile. Tommy had realised I was the legal owner of Normanby Hall and there was nothing the delegation could do about it. They would have to look elsewhere for their new residential home site.

I must admit I did feel a great sense of satisfaction as I watched the chauffeur driven limousines of our locally elected representatives depart in a rather dejected procession down the drive and off my property.

The restoration of Normanby Hall took the best part of two years and was undertaken room by room using only trusted top quality local tradesmen. A section of the roof had to be renewed but many of the original interior fixtures and fittings were saved, including the ornate ceilings, padded leather walls, oak panelling, stone and marble fireplaces and chandeliers. Some of the brickwork was unfortunately way beyond repair and had to be demolished, which left about 20 rooms for Margaret, who has impeccable taste, to design, decorate and furnish. When we eventually completed the renovations we certainly had a home of which to be proud.

Over the next few years I was fortunate enough to periodically acquire the three farms surrounding the hall but one of those purchases ended in strange and tragic circumstances.

The farm was the subject of a tenancy agreement held by two local businessmen who were brothers. After I had negotiated an appropriate price for the property I went along one afternoon to the offices of a local solicitor, Harry Simon, to sign the legal formalities and hand over a cheque for the agreed amount. As I was driving home a local news bulletin on the car radio was describing a fatal farm accident which had occurred in Normanby where a farmer had reversed his tractor over the edge of a 60 foot clay pit. Astoundingly it was the farm I'd just bought a few minutes previously and it was the occupying tenant who had unfortunately died.

After the death of her husband, which made the property freehold, I told his worried wife not to panic because she could stay in the farm for as long as she liked at a token rent of five shillings a week. Eventually the family moved on to a council estate and the property became vacant but what a tragic set of coincidences revolved around my acquisition of the farm.

After purchasing all the farmhouses, I ultimately owned a substantial tract of land totalling around 500 acres in Normanby on the outskirts of Middlesbrough, bounded by Ormesby Road to the north, Flatts Lane to the east, woodland and hillside to the south which now includes the main arterial road called the Parkway, and Cricket Lane to the west.

Today the majority of the land has been developed into top quality housing for the people of Teesside, but that development and my own formal diversification into the construction business only happened quite by chance.

Forty-five years ago when Eston Council decided to upgrade part of the Normanby sewage system one of the new branches came as far as Skippers Lane and finished directly opposite Normanby Hall. Once the "master" pipe had been positioned I gladly paid the connection charge for a further 150 yards extension from the main sewer to what is now Crathorne Park. That upgrading work meant I could not only provide the whole of my land with a proper modern drainage system but also capitalise on a marvellous business opportunity.

As a direct result of the sewer improvements my building company, Parkway Estates, was established specifically to develop the land near Normanby Hall, now known locally as Normanby Village.

In the early 1950s, once the new sewers were in place, I knew exactly how I wanted the area to look and the type of top quality housing I wanted to provide for the people of Teesside. I conveyed the detailed plans I had in my mind's eye to the well respected architect and North Riding Planning Officer Tim Thornton, who then submitted draft drawings of both a possible street layout and the housing construction. I was then able to incorporate my own original design ideas by adapting Tim's initial drawings.

The first sections of the estate to be constructed were South Park Avenue, Hollywalk Drive and Crathorne Park. We had no difficulty in selling the initial development of bungalows which I felt were competitively priced and marvellous value for money. They all sold like hot cakes.

As previously mentioned, I have always maintained a policy of building to order to avoid empty housing stock becoming a drain on my financial resources. In fact the waiting list for the first development was always over subscribed because the prospective buyers recognised the good quality housing we were erecting. Formal advertising of the properties was also kept to a minimum as the keen interest was primarily stimulated through the verbal recommendation of the new residents, which I think speaks volumes for the high standard of the construction.

My philosophy with regard to all my building work has always been to use first rate materials, to increase the legal regulations in force at a particular time by at least 50 per cent and to fit and equip the homes with the best up-to-date modern facilities available. I can honestly say I have never had one complaint about the workmanship in any of the properties built by Parkway Estates and of that statistic I am justly proud.

During the course of the 1950s and 60s, as we acquired planning permission for more land, I was able to sell certain sites at competitive prices to reputable local builders such as Cecil Yuill.

That arrangement ensured I was not only helping to provide more work for the local economy, but it also guaranteed a greater variety of housing stock would be constructed to attract new prospective buyers to what was a pleasant semi-rural environment.

As I now look at the 1,000 homes which have been built on my land over the last 40 years I must admit to feeling a great sense of personal satisfaction and achievement that I have, even in a small way, contributed towards improving the quality of life for the people of my home area.

Running parallel with the restoration of the main house I also returned the grounds of Normanby Hall to their former glory, which was no mean task considering many of the outbuildings had fallen into a state of disrepair and the undergrowth had taken on jungle proportions. I employed two full-time gardeners to undertake the work and during the whole process of renovation I felt I was preserving a part of the Teesside's local heritage for posterity and that seemed a very worthwhile endeavour.

The rural environment certainly provided me with an opportunity to develop new and diverse business ideas based around the estate and one of my first projects was to build a piggery on the side of the walled garden. For a considerable time we kept over 600 pigs which we bred and sold on every month to a dealer in Darlington, who believe it or not was called Mr Pigg.

As with most new ventures in my life I was very keen to familiarise myself with all aspects of the operation and in particular I studied the most cost effective pig farming production methods.

One of the early problems I encountered was a high level of piglet fatality caused by the sow rolling over and crushing the piglets while they were suckling. After initially seeking advice about the occurrence it quickly became apparent there was no guaranteed method of reducing the losses, it was purely down to trial and error.

During my background research into the problem, however, I did read an article in a farming magazine which claimed the piglet fatality rate could be cut if the design of the stys was altered and they were heated with infra-red lighting. The theory claimed the warmer environment reduced the movement of the sow and with it the likelihood of crushing the offsprings.

The notion seemed to be quite enterprising and as far as I was concerned any original idea which reduced my piglet loss was worth pursuing. I therefore decided to investigate the practical possibilities of introducing a similar method of pig-rearing to Normanby Hall.

The new approach was being pioneered at Luton Hoo, the impressive 18th Century home of the Wernher family, who had initiated diamond mining in South Africa in the 19th Century.

The estate had been bought in 1903 by Sir Julius Wernher as a place to exhibit the family's fabulous art collection.

At that particular time in the late 1940s I was involved in dubbing the soundtrack for the film Holiday Camp for Gainsborough Pictures at Lime Grove Studios and after one of the sessions in London I took a detour to Luton Hoo in Bedfordshire with Eric Davison and Howard Kershaw to investigate the novel pig farming experiment.

As we neared Luton Hoo we found ourselves on a long tree-lined driveway which carried on for a distance of at least half a mile.

Fearing we'd taken a wrong turning I stopped to ask directions from a man dressed rather shabbily in felt hat and worn raincoat who was walking along the track. I explained to him we were looking for the piggeries at Luton Hoo and he very politely informed us we were in fact on the right road. Then, pointing with his walking stick, he told us to carry on up the drive until we came to a barred gate. We were to leave the car there and walk to the outbuildings and ask for the pig farm manager who would see to our request.

As we proceeded up the tree-lined drive we saw in the distance a stunning mansion house set in 1,500 acres of vast parkland. Opening the barred gate we were captivated by the splendour of the surroundings. It was a truly magnificent setting in which to live.

We were warmly received by the farm manager who was very willing to share the information about the infra red lighting technique they were pioneering. When I first saw the piggeries I was astounded at the quality and cleanliness of the modern outbuildings. Some of the digs I'd stayed in when touring with the band would have been hard pushed to emulate those conditions.

It was patently obvious, even to my inexperienced eye, that the animals were very secure in their warm environment and because of that apparent contentment, the incidence of piglet fatality had been drastically reduced.

I was treated with great kindness and courtesy by the farm manager. Nothing was too much trouble for him and after he'd answered all my questions, we were told the owner of the estate wished to see us before we left.

We were taken into the impressive drawing room of the mansion house and while we were admiring the sumptuous decor, the door opened and to our total amazement and surprise in walked the man wearing the felt hat who had given us the directions on the driveway. I couldn't believe we'd asked for assistance from the present owner of Luton Hoo, Sir Harold Wernher, who all through our roadside conversation had remained incognito. At least Sir Harold had a sense of humour and saw the funny side of our embarrassing situation.

Sir Harold offered all of us a glass of sherry and I found him to be a very modest, helpful and courteous man. He told us Luton Hoo had originally been built in 1767 by Robert Adam for the Earl of Bute but had been destroyed by fire and rebuilt in 1843. The surrounding parkland had been landscaped by the famous designer Capability Brown and the mansion housed many art treasures, including Faberge mementos of the Russian Imperial Family.

He also listened very intently to my plans for the piggeries at Normanby Hall and even suggested the best pig breeding stock in the northern area was to be bought at a farm near Bridlington in North Yorkshire, which sold very lean Land Race Boars. Armed with that useful breeding information I thanked him very much for being so generous with his time and I left with a great deal more porcine knowledge than when I'd arrived.

We eventually adapted Luton Hoo's infra red lighting system at Normanby Hall and it was a marvellous success. The heat produced by the lights meant our sows were kept warm and contented and less agitated, which meant the piglets were much safer when they were suckling.

Acting on Sir Harold's information about breeding stock we arranged to buy a boar from the farm he'd recommended near Bridlington. But transporting the animal back to Teesside resembled something akin to a Buster Keaton silent comedy caper.

We paid £40 for a ten week old young boar and fully expected we would be provided with a small crate in which to transport him safely home. To my surprise, however, the farmer asked us how far we were travelling. When we said about 60 miles to Middlesbrough he told us the pig would be fine just tied up in a hessian sack and placed on the back seat of the car.

For the whole of the return journey to our piggeries the young boar did its darnest to extricate itself from the sack by kicking, squealing and fighting. What a din. There were times coming across the moors road I thought he was about to escape and join me in the passenger seat.

To give credit where it is due, he eventually turned out to be a fine acquisition, growing to a weight of nearly half a ton and providing us with many saleable litters.

At the same time as I was expanding the piggeries I also built a 90 foot long greenhouse in which to cultivate a small market garden. The idea behind the innovation was to provide the Coatham Hotel in Redcar with fresh produce such as tomatoes. Now I've always adopted the attitude during my life that if you are going to build something, then build it big, but in the case of the greenhouse we were so successful we had 800 pounds of tomatoes just from one crop. We couldn't give them away and ended up feeding most of them to the pigs.

Another one of my short lived agricultural business ideas was to cultivate some of the arable land by growing wheat and potatoes. The fields, however, were too close to the local housing estates and the crops were often damaged or deliberately removed, so I decided it wasn't worth the time or the effort to pursue a part-time career in farming.

We also kept 400 white leghorn hens on the estate, again with the idea of being self sufficient by servicing the Coatham Hotel with eggs and white meat.

When we were erecting the coops I was advised to dig down at least a couple of feet and place the mesh underground to limit the possibility of fox attacks. But even that precautionary measure still failed to stop a fox from tunnelling under the fencing one night and killing over 100 of our hens. The scene when I arrived the next day was very depressing. It was one of utter carnage. The fox had just run amok and had obviously been killing the birds just for fun. There were dismembered carcasses of dead and dying birds strewn all over the ground. It was a pitiful sight. We set a trap for the culprit and eventually caught and shot it.

One of my favourite purchases in the 1950s was a heavy horse called a Clydesdale. We acquired her from a farmer in Great Ayton and what a magnificent gentle beast she was. I originally bought her as a working horse to pull a block cart around the estate transporting rubble or manure to wherever it was required.

In fact she was involved in proving my eldest son Kevan could be just as enterprising as his father, when one afternoon near Christmas both he and the horse went missing.

We searched everywhere on the estate for them, but to no avail. We were becoming very worried when finally, an hour and half later, we saw the horse clip clopping up the lane with 12-year-old Kevan and his friend sitting on top of an empty cart smiling broadly.

After we'd chastised him, it transpired he'd been cutting down numerous sprigs of holly from the trees in the grounds of Normanby Hall and had then trotted up and down the local neighbourhood selling them from the cart as Christmas decorations. Although he did receive a sound telling off for the upset he'd caused, I did very much admire his young entrepreneurial spirit. A real chip off the old Amer block.

A Clydesdale horse is very much a working animal but Margaret could never come to terms with that fact. She treated the horse as a pet. One day she even suggested I was over-working the animal when she saw its bulging muscles pulling a fully laden cartload of rubble. She remonstrated with me, saying I should be ashamed of myself for allowing the horse to struggle with such a heavy load. Soon after our mild disagreement I sold the offending cart but kept the horse.

In the mid 1950s the same Clydesdale mare gave me one of the most enthralling and amazing experiences of my life.

One day as I approached her in the pasture I noticed something pure white attached to her hind quarters. As I got closer I realised she was delivering a foal, so I quickly ran back to the house and phoned for some veterinary help. I was informed the occurrence was surprising as most Clydesdale births usually happened at night under cover of darkness.

When I returned to the field the pure white sac containing the foal was already on the ground.

I was totally captivated by the deeply moving event that was unexpectedly unfolding before my eyes. The mare lowered her head and bit open the sac to release a beautiful foal whose first instant reaction was to stagger to its feet on unsteady rubbery legs, while its proud mother lovingly licked it dry.

It was a wonderful experience to be present at the beginning of a new life.

Although we eventually restored Normanby Hall to its former glory there's a conundrum we've never managed to solve, and that's the mystery of the secret room.

Its exact location was discovered purely by chance in the 1950s when we were taking a lead from a power point in a ground floor corridor to the upstairs sitting room. As we drilled a hole in the ceiling and pushed yards and yards of cable through, no end appeared. Puzzled by the occurrence I took some internal structural measurements and found one of the walls was in fact partitioned.

Removing the floorboards, I shone my flashlight through the gap. There on the floor in the gloom was an amazing sight - thousands of documents and newspapers, systematically stacked and neatly tied up with string, their edges brown and crinkled but all still beautifully preserved. A real relic of the past.

On closer examination we estimated the material covered a period of over 200 years and provided an historical time capsule of 18th and 19th century England.

Detailed information and data was chronicled on a variety of printed ephemera including national and local newspapers, monthly reviews, Parliamentary and Government papers, military documents, court proceedings and English literature pamphlets. To discover so much hidden material relating to the life and times of the hall's former occupants was a fascinating experience.

I spent many enlightening hours perusing the wonderfully colourful and formal language contained in the material. With no mass media in those days, written communication had to be vivid, descriptive and evocative to provide the reader with an accurate account of the events of that time at both home and abroad.

It would have been the only way the population received any information and although modern technology has developed rapidly, it is worth noting the day to day worries of people have remained the same as the Whitehall Evening Post of 1830 complained in its headline, "The grinding effects of taxation", which only goes to prove some things never change. Interestingly a 1784 copy of the Newcastle Chronicle gave notice on its back page of a State Lottery with a first prize of £20,000. Again so much for contemporary originality.

While reading, I also came to realise how quickly we have conveniently forgotten that less than 300 years ago, far from being a civilised country, our people were often being hung, drawn, quartered and decapitated while they were still alive and all apparently in the name of justice. Graphic descriptions of barbaric activities proliferate some of the gruesome copy of the early newspapers.

Taking the document dates as a general indicator, most of the items must have been brought to the present hall when it was reconstructed in 1812, but why they were hidden from view in the middle of the 19th Century, one can only speculate.

Around that time in 1854, George Edwin Jackson died, but his brothers the Reverend William and Ralph Jackson lived until 1874 and 1880 respectively and some of their papers were also found among the material we discovered. So, exactly why the secret room was constructed and sealed with an upper class family's history remains shrouded in mystery. Who knows, it may have been a deliberate act rather like today's contemporary artifacts which are interred in a variety of time capsules for future generations to learn about the past.

Whatever the reasons, it was a marvellous surprise to discover them after all those years and in such wonderful condition. They certainly opened up a window on the past and their sale created a good deal of interest from collectors and historians when they were auctioned at Christies in London.

In 1974 I was deeply saddened when Normanby Hall was burgled and my fine collection of silver was stolen. When somebody enters your home without permission it feels as though your personal space has been violated and it takes a long time before you can come to terms with the distressing circumstances of that violation. I was both deeply upset and angry by the loss of a collection which had taken me 36 years to accumulate, beginning with a small cigarette case presented to me before the war by some of the appreciative campers at Skegness.

I'm afraid I will never understand the confused mentality which lives by the principle of, if you haven't got it, you steal it. In my mind there is no situation or justification for people to resort to stealing the possessions of others. Personal pride is only achieved through the acquisition of something you have worked hard for and often struggled to buy. It is not obtained through any form of criminal activity.

A 34-year-old thief, who had gained entry to the hall by forcing the kitchen window and removing the silver from the lounge, was later apprehended and charged with trespassing and burglary. For committing the offence he quite rightly received a custodial sentence. I am also pleased to say all the silver, apart from two pieces, was located in the Midlands about two months after the crime and returned to us in good condition, thus providing a positive postscript to the unfortunate episode.

CHAPTER SEVEN

Right place, right time

All through my business and private life I have consciously endeavoured to treat people fairly and with courtesy. Those are the principles and sentiments I have also fastidiously conveyed to my sons Kevan and Philip and I am immensely proud of what they've achieved in a variety of business ventures.

People have often asked me if there is a secret formula which can guarantee business success. The answer, however, is quite simple. There are no short cuts, only hard work and determination. Nothing more nothing less. The world doesn't owe anyone a living and not everybody is fortunate enough to be a million pounds winner on the football pools or the national lottery.

So my down to earth advice would be if you want to achieve anything in life, you must clearly identify your intended objective, then be totally dedicated in order to achieve that goal, and be prepared to work long hours with people on whom you can trust and depend.

There's an old saying which still stands the test of time today: "It's not what you know, but who you know". Drawing on my own multifarious experiences over the last 60 years, I'd certainly endorse that observation. Business success can often hinge or depend on your ability as an individual to foster, cultivate and retain both friendships and relationships with other professional people.

Occasionally, however, opportunities present themselves because you are very fortunate and happen to be in the right place at the right time rather than possessing any intuitive business skill or acumen, as the next series of reminiscences perfectly illustrates. They begin with a fortuitous meeting in the autumn of 1942.

I was working in my office at the Palais de Danse in Skinner Street, Stockton-on-Tees, when there was a robust knock on the door. As I shouted 'Come In', a tall rather impressive man, confidently entered the room and asked if it would be possible to make an important telephone call, as his line in the adjacent office building appeared to be dead. Without hesitation I granted the polite request.

When he'd finished his conversation, I noticed his attention was drawn to a bottle of whisky on the shelf behind my desk. Out of courtesy I offered him a drink. I was pouring the Haig carefully into a glass when the penny dropped and I suddenly realised who he was.

As he slowly and contentedly sipped the malt, he invited me for a meal to Freddie Bowman's Black Lion Grill Room in Stockton High Street. I gladly accepted the invitation and lunched with Harold Macmillan, the future Conservative Prime Minister and Stockton's Member of Parliament for nearly 20 years from 1924 to 1945. What a pleasant man he was and how well informed, because during our discourse he asked me how my ENSA band concerts were progressing.

I told him we were experiencing more than a little difficulty in fulfiling some of our engagements, due to the acute shortage of fuel caused by the strict enforcement of petrol rationing.

He was very sympathetic with regard to my predicament and fully acknowledged the morale boosting work we were doing for ENSA. As we parted he kindly promised to investigate the possibility of obtaining additional petrol for me.

I must admit I didn't think any more about the conversation until a short time later I received an official letter personally signed by Harold Macmillan. The contents informed me he'd been in touch with Mr Geoffrey Lloyd MP, the Parliamentary Secretary at the Ministry of Fuel and Power, about acquiring a supplementary petrol allowance for our cars, and in view of the essential morale boosting nature of our work an enhanced ration would be made. He had been as good as his word.

Less than a week later, a thick buff envelope arrived at my office containing the extra petrol coupons and a contact number in Newcastle to ring for a further supply when they ran out. What a help those coupons were in ensuring the band arrived at their gigs. And to think it all happened because of a chance meeting when the local MP's telephone line had gone dead.

Another example of making an acquaintance in the most unexpected of circumstances occurred when I was bizarrely prosecuted for buying and fitting a wooden dance floor in the Corporation Hall in Prince Regent Street, Stockton-on-Tees.

During the war years there were very strict licences issued for the purchasing of certain commodities which were in short supply or classified as important items, and timber came into that category.

I'd wanted to upgrade the Corporation Hall's poor flooring for some time. So, after making many enquiries, I thought I'd finally circumnavigated the bureaucracy and red tape when I located a portable dance floor stored in a Newcastle upon Tyne warehouse. It was in marvellous condition, made from solid oak and was exactly what I required for the refurbishment.

Once it was reassembled in Stockton, we screwed it securely to the concrete floor of the hall and I must say when we'd finished, it was a rather grand and very professional looking surface. But if there's one thing I've learned over the years it's never to become too complacent in business because no sooner had we completed the renovation than the problems began.

A short while later I had a visit from a very personable man called Mr Nicholson who went under the rather grand title of the Regional Licensing Officer. He told me I'd been reported to his office in Newcastle for buying timber without the correct and proper authorisation. Of course I vociferously protested my innocence, believing I'd done nothing underhand and I willingly showed him the relevant paperwork appertaining to the purchase. He agreed the documents were in order but pointed out that unfortunately the floor was not being used for its designated purpose, in other words a portable dance floor. It was now a fixed floor and therefore contravened the technical licensing regulations. I couldn't believe what I was hearing, because I'd secured the floor to the concrete I was going to be prosecuted on a legal technicality.

The officer seemed genuinely apologetic and agreed there appeared to be no deliberate intent on my behalf to break the regulations but unfortunately rules were rules. He'd apparently been acting on an anonymous tip off (I had my suspicions as to the identity of the culprit) and therefore I was to be charged with purchasing timber without the appropriate and relevant licence. I informed my solicitor Tommy Jackson who advised me to plead guilty, and because I had unintentionally broken the law and had co-operated fully with the investigation, he thought I would just receive a small fine.

COLONIAL OFFICE,

DOWNING STREET, S.W.1.

5th November, 1942.

Dear Mr. Amer,

    I have been in touch with Mr. Geoffrey Lloyd, M.P., the Parliamentary Secretary at the Ministry of Fuel and Power, about the question of a petrol allowance for one of your cars. I have just got a letter from Mr. Lloyd telling me that a petrol allowance is now to be made for one car.

    I am very glad to have had the opportunity of helping you in this way.

    Yours sincerely,

    Harold Macmillan.

Charles Amer, Esq.

The official letter sent to me by Harold Macmillan confirming the acquisition of extra fuel for my ENSA work.

I duly appeared before Stockton magistrates, pleaded guilty as advised, and was ready to pay my nominal fine when one of the magistrates insisted the bench should retire to consider the case more thoroughly in private. When they eventually emerged from their deliberations I was informed my fine was a swingeing £50 (around £500 today). I was totally flabbergasted, but could do nothing. I had to accept the judgement.

As we left the court Mr Nicholson and his assistant came over to commiserate with me, saying he thought the fine bordered on the excessive and I had to concur with his assessment. I told him not to worry, I appreciated he'd only been carrying out his duties and I asked him if he would like to have lunch with me. He was totally amazed I should want to buy a meal for the person who was responsible for my court appearance. But I had no axe to grind with him, although I did have the feeling certain faceless members of the local community were not entirely 100% behind my expanding business ventures.

After our meal at Freddie Bowman's we parted the best of friends and Mr Nichloson suggested if I required any help in the future I was to give him a ring in Newcastle.

Little did I know I would be calling on his advice sooner than I anticipated when in late 1945 the authorities permitted Bill Butlin to re-open part of the Filey camp. By utilising Mr Nicholson's professional assistance we were able to swiftly acquire the relevant licences in order to purchase the building materials we needed to convert the military site back into a holiday camp. Without his expertise I doubt whether the facilities would have been available as quickly as they were, which only serves to emphasise the merit of retaining your business contacts because you never know when they may be required.

In December 1944 a chance meeting at a local seaside resort began a whole chain of events which eventually lead to my serious involvement in the hotel and catering trade.

I had initially gone to Redcar with a friend of mine, Jack Coffield, to view the old pier ballroom in the hope of finding a new venue to cater for the large potential audience in that part of Teesside. I'd been reliably informed the ballroom was for sale, but we were disappointed to find the property was in fact not on the market as it was the subject of a compulsory purchase order from Redcar Council.

On our way home we stopped at the Coatham Hotel for some liquid refreshment and as I ordered the drinks the barman recognised me as a local band leader and asked me what I was doing in Redcar.

The promenade at Redcar with the Coatham Hotel standing impressively on the seafront circa 1930.

When I told him I'd been hoping to buy the pier ballroom he informed me, rather bluntly, I wasn't going to have it. Quite taken aback by his authoritative abruptness I politely enquired why he was so sure of his facts.

I must admit I did laugh at his reply when he told me in his official capacity as the local mayor he knew for certain the council were going to buy the venue. I couldn't grumble. At least I'd heard the explanation from the horse's mouth.

Sidney Shillito then seriously suggested if I was so keen on opening a new venue in Redcar I should view the hotel's ballroom which had been closed since being used as a billet for Canadian and Czech airforce personnel during the war. As we walked through the hotel corridors I noticed most of the main rooms comprised of temporary partitions which were sectioned off to provide the living quarters. Those areas were littered with the discarded debris and rubbish of their former residents who had obviously made a quick exit back to their homelands.

When I once again viewed the spacious hotel ballroom - I'd played there before the war with Charlie Skinner - I knew instinctively that the venue had unlimited potential. And even though the affects of swilling had made the superb maplewood dance floor slightly warped it was certainly not beyond repair. The overall problem, however, was the likely purchase price, which I thought would probably be way beyond the limit of my financial resources at that time.

I was initially looking for a long-term lease on the ballroom, so adopting the principle of nothing ventured nothing gained, I attended a meeting with the hotel secretary and accountant Clive Gilden, but was informed the shareholders were more interested in selling the entire hotel rather than leasing part of it.

I therefore entered exploratory discussions on that basis, the outcomes of which were very positive and it was eventually decided the hotel's directors would sell their shares to me for a reasonable price. I was convinced the premises had potential and it was a business opportunity not to be missed.

In order to raise the venture capital for the purchase of the Coatham Hotel, the Corporation Hall in Stockton was bought by the local council and I sold 40 per cent of my own hotel shareholding to other trusted business associates.

I was assisted in meeting one of those business associates by the divine intervention of a sheep, which I know sounds extremely far fetched but believe me the incident I am about to recount is perfectly true.

I was travelling across the North Yorkshire Moors on the A174 back to Butlin's Holiday Camp in Filey, where I was living at the time, for an evening concert with my orchestra, when suddenly and without warning, a sheep darted out of the heather in front of my car. I had little chance of avoiding the wayward animal and as we collided my vehicle veered off the road and became lodged in a ditch.

Fortunately there were no dry stone walls in the vicinity and I escaped unhurt, albeit a little shaken. Fellow passing motorists were most kind and stopped to offer assistance but the car was stuck fast and I eventually had to phone my brother-in-law to organise its recovery. Left with no transport, arriving on time for the band's show seemed out of the question but I needn't have worried because as often happens in times of crisis, somebody always comes to your rescue. The Good Samaritan on this occasion was a solicitor from Middlesbrough called Harry Simon who generously volunteered to drive me to Butlin's so I wouldn't miss the concert.

Just as we were about to set off for Filey the sheep, which I'd presumed was dead because it had been motionless since the solid impact, suddenly sprang to life, gingerly shook itself, gave out a large bleat, staggered a few steps as if intoxicated, and then sprinted away like a bat out of hell over the moors, seemingly none the worse for our impromptu meeting. I must admit to feeling a sense of relief at its revival because I hate to see animals suffer.

As we drove to Filey I chatted freely to Harry Simon about my involvement with the band and it coincidentally transpired he also had a very keen interest in the entertainment world, forming numerous friendships with the stars of that era. During our general conversation I spoke about my business expansion plans and the proposed acquisition of the Coatham Hotel and its great potential.

On hearing my outline plans for the Coatham, Simon quite unexpectedly enquired if it would be possible for him to invest in the proposed development.

Later, and after more detailed discussions, Harry Simon became a shareholder in the Coatham. So, thanks to the wayward meanderings of a moorland sheep, we began a friendship which lasted for over 30 years and I had enough capital to buy the hotel.

But that wasn't the end of the story. When the final transactions were complete I was pleased to find the hotel's bank account contained a £10,000 windfall which was an insurance payment for bomb damage which had occurred during the war. That unexpected financial bonus enabled me to start the much needed refurbishment work almost immediately, and the hotel paid for itself within a year of me taking over.

During the next decade I developed the hotel ballroom into the prime dance venue in the Teesside area. No doubt many of you reading this book will have spent numerous happy evenings there gliding across the floor to the melodies played by the Charles Amer Orchestra. In fact to this day, married couples still confide in me that they met at one of my dances and jest that I was responsible, if not to blame, for their resulting nuptials.

The development of the Coatham was rapid. We added another wing, called the Windsor Ballroom, which we built to match the original Victorian limestone facade. I also began booking the very best in top quality entertainment like Geraldo and his Orchestra who I'd met through my work with ENSA.

Coincidently, in the late 1940s and early 1950s there was also a significant upsurge in the industrial expansion of Teesside with firms like ICI investing heavily in the area. But there was a dearth of first class hotel accommodation for business executives.

Recognising that need, I managed to negotiate an extended block booking from ICI for all rooms the on the Coatham's top floor, which were to be permanently available for any of their visiting personnel. That ideal arrangement provided me with a source of stable income and fostered good public relations whether the rooms were occupied or not.

By the early 1950s I had fully established the Coatham Hotel's reputation for live dance music and had also helped to develop a Mecca for the devotees of jazz, with the creation of the famous Redcar Jazz Club. That milestone in local entertainment eventually gained national acclaim for its excellence in a genre which had previously been viewed as a minority and rather elitist pastime. The club's formation was an original innovation and its success gave me much personal satisfaction.

The embryonic club evolved when a number of keen local pub based musicians and enthusiasts, who needed a larger venue, approached me to rent the Coatham's small ballroom. Their idea appealed to me but I suggested they should perhaps utilise the facilities of the larger Windsor ballroom in tandem with some of my own dance band members, such as Dickie Hunter, Howard Kershaw and Bill Walker, who wished to indulge themselves by performing in their own jazz group. I am pleased to say my suggestion was accepted and a permanent base for the Redcar Jazz Club was established.

I wish to emphasise the future success of the club had little to do with my involvement. The plaudits and accolades for the superb organisation should be given in particular to Bob Armstong and the hard working and dedicated committee members who at various times included, Mike Lawson, Harry Atterton, Rodger Barker, Ron Hall, Geoff Oldroyd and Eric Wilkinson.

The popularity of the club's Sunday evening gigs was quickly established within the local area and visitors were impressed with the facilities, friendliness and welcoming atmosphere of the venue. We provided a full waitress service and during the club's hey-day it wasn't unusual for enthusiasts to make sure of their admission by queuing on the promenade from the late afternoon until the doors opened at 6.30pm.

During the Fifties and early Sixties the reputation of the club became synonymous with jazz excellence. As word spread about the quality and popularity of the venue, London agents began visiting the club. They liked what they saw and that seal of approval gradually ensured that all the famous bands and musicians of the period played at the Coatham, including

Bob Wallis and the Storyville Jazzmen play for another packed house at the famous Redcar Jazz Club which was based in the Windsor Ballroom at the Coatham Hotel.

Johnny Dankworth and Cleo Lane, Acker Bilk, Eric Delaney, Terry Lightfoot, Alex Welsh, Ronnie Scott and American legends such as Henry "Red" Allen. The list of established performers was endless.

At the time we probably didn't realise how influential the club was in the shaping of jazz appreciation, not only in the North-east, but also in the country as a whole. I have since come to realise when listening to people's affectionate recollections of that period, what a significant part the jazz club played in the cultural development of the Teesside area and how much the members anticipated their Sunday evenings in Redcar.

In a recent local history publication it has been claimed the club was a venue for unseemly behaviour such as drug taking. Those preposterous accusations are not true. When I sold the Coatham in 1963 the formal jazz club was still in existence. But later in the 1960s the venue itself was infiltrated by the new pop culture and the title of the Redcar Jazz Club was misused to describe the electric guitar "music" then being played. That offshoot should never have been confused with the original club which was an organisation efficiently run for the members by the members and any attempt to devalue their notable achievements does them a great disservice.

Redcar Jazz Club chairman Bob Armstrong, left, and president Ron Hall, right, assist Wilf Proudfoot MP with a prize draw in the Windsor Ballroom at the Coatham Hotel.

In the catering trade you are always trying to develop new and innovative ideas to stimulate business and one my most successful ventures involved the local ethnic community.

After World War Two, the Teesside area had a large, thriving and very hardworking Italian population which was mostly based in and around the ice-cream making industry. The firms were mainly owned by closely knit families such as Rea's, Rossi's, Greco's, Lanny's, Salvatore's and Paleschi's.

In the late 1940s I responded keenly to a request from the Rea brothers, Cammilo and Coya, to use the Coatham Hotel's Windsor Ballroom for a new social event specifically catering for the Italian community. The evening was later affectionately referred to as the 'Ice Cream Ball'.

When the first formal ball was advertised it proved to be so popular that it was immediately oversubscribed and had a long waiting list for tickets. After the inaugural success, which was due entirely to the boundless energy, enthusiasm and organisational skills displayed by Cammilo and Coya Rea, the grand function became established as one of the most eagerly anticipated annual events on the local social calendar, with its popularity continuing for well over a decade.

As a result of that popularity we later expanded the original idea into a Neopolitan Evening, so that other members of the public could experience the charming delights of Italian culture and cuisine. Again Cammilo and Coya Rea were involved in the organisation and for many years, beginning at the Coatham and later at the Marton Hotel and Country Club, we successfully catered for upwards of 300 people at a time.

Some of the patrons who attended those functions had never eaten spaghetti before, and watching their often hilarious attempts to consume the main course was worth the ticket money alone.

They say it's an ill wind that blows nobody any good. Well, after the events of January 1952, I'm afraid I'd have to totally disagree.

I was returning from the printer's along a windswept Redcar promenade near Turner Street when I suddenly became aware of a ship's outline looming out of the sea mist, about 200 yards offshore. I remember thinking to myself, 'For goodness sake I hope you've stopped or you're going to demolish the Coatham Hotel'. The ship in question was the 4,221 ton Greek merchantman Taxiarchis which had run aground in gale force winds on the infamous Red Scar rocks, which in their time had been the scene of many a maritime disaster in the Tees Bay.

Another Italian evening goes with a swing as Coya Rea, centre, leads left to right, Freddie McManus, Cammilo Rea, Joe Paleschi, Charles Amer, Dr Jack Evans and Mazzi de Palma in an impromptu sing-song.

Initially the captain and the 27 crew members pluckily stayed on board for two days in the vain hope that the vessel could be refloated. But when the weather rapidly deteriorated, flooding the engine room and two of her holds, they were persuaded that the right course of action was to abandon their ship.

The officers stayed with us in the Coatham Hotel while the ship was stuck fast for over a month, stubbornly defying all attempts by the tugboats to move her.

Eventually, when it was obvious she was going to flounder, the decision was made to sell her for scrap to the Sheffield firm of iron merchants Thomas Ward Ltd, but not before she became quite a local tourist attraction. It never ceases to amaze me how human nature is drawn like a magnet to adversity, because literally thousands of sightseers came down to the seafront to gawp at the poor stricken vessel.

My eldest son Kevan, who was in his early teens at the time, also became fascinated by the ship and asked me if it would be possible to climb on board to have a look around. I must say the thought of scrambling up the side of the ship on small rope ladders did not appeal to me at all, but I agreed to pursue the possibility just to satisfy his curiosity.

During the salvage operation I had become very friendly with the Lloyds inspectors and various shipping agents who were also based at the Coatham Hotel and they kindly gave me permission to take Kevan onboard the Taxiarchis.

I took some of my building workers to assist me and we all watched Kevan climb, like an agile monkey, up the rope ladder which was draped rather pathetically over the rusting bow.

When it was my turn, I insisted on having a strong line tightly secured around my waist for extra insurance before I made my slow and very tentative ascent up the ageing hull.

Once on the listing deck of the relatively small ship I was still struck by how high we were above the rocks. As we walked around her, I happened to notice the hold covers were wide open and peering down into the cavernous depths of the ship's interior, I saw hundreds of lengths of new timber, some of which were floating on top of the ballast water.

Kevan thought his adventure on board ship was marvellous but I was already more concerned about the eventual fate of the timber cargo.

On my return to the Coatham I asked the Lloyds inspectors about the destiny of the wood. I was told, given the right price, it might be surplus to requirements but legally it had to be initially offered for sale to any local timber merchants who were interested. I requested to be kept fully informed of all the developments, but in my mind I was already planning to extend the piggeries at Normanby Hall.

After about ten days it became apparent that none of the local timber merchants were interested in salvaging the material because of the logistical problems involved in its removal. Seizing my opportunity I quickly agreed an acceptable price for all the wood on board, but the practical problems of salvage and storage were only just beginning.

What seemed to have been a good idea at the time rapidly turned into a nightmare. Because of the vagaries of the tides and the slow pace of work, emptying the four holds took nearly three weeks, much longer than I had anticipated. Every length of timber was individually hauled out of the hold and then painstakingly lowered down the side of the ship on to the waiting lorries and transported to the large carpark at the Coatham Hotel to be stockpiled. Eventually, because there was so much timber, we ran out of space and I had to transfer the remainder of the salvage to be stacked at the rear of Normanby Hall. The operation developed into a mammoth task.

The ill-fated Taxiarchis, stranded on the rocks at Redcar in January 1952, proved to be a very profitable ship for me.

We eventually removed a quite staggering 40 tons of unwanted timber from the hold of the Taxiarchis and then we only had the small problem of selling it.

I decided to keep some for my own building work but I was still left with a huge amount of saleable timber for which I needed an outlet.

At that juncture I was still performing with my band at Butlin's Holiday Camp, Filey. I was also very friendly with Frank Cusworth who was in overall charge of holiday camp development and site expansion for Bill Butlin and one afternoon he came on social visit to Normanby Hall.

As we walked through the grounds he noticed the drying timber piled high at the back of the house and enquired if there was any material to spare. Only a carpark full, I thought to myself.

To precis the outcome of the story, Butlin's eventually purchased all the surplus wood from the shipwreck for their expansion programme of the Skegness and Pwllheli camps. I made a handsome return on my nautical investment and the satisfactory conclusion to the episode only serves to highlight how business opportunities can arise in the most unexpected of circumstances.

The ill-fated Taxiarchis was stuck so fast on the rocks that the operation to break her up took the best part of seven months - but she proved to be a very profitable ship indeed for me.

Many of the football teams playing Middlesbrough after the war stayed at the Coatham Hotel. Here I'm pictured with a Liverpool team which contained Bob Paisley, standing at the back of the group.

As a consequence of the successful salvage operation I became acquainted with the managing director of TW Ward's and a few months later he rang to enquire if I would be interested in purchasing any of the high quality fixtures and fittings from an ocean going liner which was to be broken up at the Inverkeithing yard in Scotland.

Naturally I accepted the invitation. The excursion involved me taking a launch right out to sea to survey the ship's contents before she docked and marking any of the items which I thought would be of interest.

As I boarded the liner on a lowered gangway, I was astounded by what confronted me. She was a floating palace and, having been used by the Royal Family on a state visit to Canada in the 1930s, the fixtures and fittings were of the highest quality. In fact they were positively luxurious. I was particularly attracted to the solid oak panelling on the walls but some of the tables and chairs in the main lounges were also items of great value and style.

In the end I identified so many items I had to hire three lorries to carry all the furniture, including a grand piano, back to Teesside. The majority of the material found a good home in the Coatham Hotel in Redcar, so if you ever attended one of my functions at the hotel in the 1950's there was a distinct possibility you may have sat on some of the royal furniture purchased from that liner.

Another example of good fortune or lady luck, call it what you will, happened at Normanby Hall in the early 1950s and involved my gardener Fred, who was digging in the enclosed garden near the main house. As he thrust his spade into the ground he struck a hard metallic object. On closer investigation we uncovered a silver lead pipe about three inches in diameter. Now lead was, and still is, a very valuable metal so I suggested to Fred he should follow the pipe to its source and left him to carry on the excavation. The garden measured an acre and half so there was a good deal of strenuous spade work to be done.

A few days later, after I'd returned home from Butlin's on a day visit, I went to look at the piggeries and enquired about Fred's progress.

"He's still digging, Mr Amer, like you told him to," I was informed by Harry, his assistant.

"What do you mean, he's still digging?" I asked, not quite grasping the finer details of the explanation.

"Up there in the woods," he replied, with a smile on his face and pointing in the general direction of the hillside.

I followed Fred's immaculately cut trench for about half a mile to the top of the woods behind Normanby Hall where I discovered the lead pipe originated from a small forgotten reservoir which was fed by local springs. In days gone by the reservoir had supplied the house with water before I'd connected the property to the mains. The hundreds of yards of lead piping was of course now obsolete, so I had it all removed and we sold the white metal for a very tidy and unexpected profit. It was literally an example of buried treasure.

CHAPTER EIGHT

Hotels and Roundabouts

The 1960s were a period of considerable change in my life, beginning with a full recovery from major abdominal surgery. In 1963 I sold the Coatham Hotel, which at the time had more en suite facilities than any other hotel in the North-east to Youngers Brewery for a suitably advantageous price. I also purchased the sites where the Marton Hotel and Country Club in Middlesbrough and The York Hotel in Redcar now stand, began to wind down the live appearances made by the orchestra, and became a director of Middlesbrough Football Club.

For nearly 25 years my hectic professional life had at various times consisted of summer seasons at Butlin's, constant winter touring with my orchestra, developing my building interests through Parkway Estates, undertaking charity work on behalf of the Variety Club and organising numerous social functions in the local dance halls and theatres around the Teesside area. During that whole period I had never stopped, sometimes working 16 hours a day, seven days a week without a holiday because I enjoyed my lifestyle so much.

Meal times were irregular and often snatched when convenient, causing me to suffer from a persistent stomach irritation. In fact one day it became so acute that the mother of one of the gardeners at Filey noticed my ashen face and suggested I ate some molasses to ease the condition. The alternative remedy appeared to pacify the problem until early in 1960 when I suddenly collapsed in the Coatham Hotel with excruciating abdominal pains. My GP at the time, Dr. Wally Davies, thought in all probability I had an ulcer. I refused to be treated on Teesside because I was still saddened by the poor quality of care my mother had received just after the war when, after undergoing routine surgery at the Eston Cottage Hospital, she unexpectedly died of post operative shock.

I therefore travelled by train to Harley Street in London for exhaustive tests. From there I was transferred to the Westminster Hospital where they diagnosed I had three acutely developed ulcers which needed immediate emergency treatment before my condition became critical.

I returned to Teesside, telling my family nothing about the gravity of my condition. In order not to cause them any undue worry or alarm I told them the doctors' in London wanted to carry out further tests to establish a more specific diagnosis.

My operation, which was observed by 20 American specialists, was undertaken by a consultant surgeon called Mr Frank de A'breu and resulted in the removal of over half my stomach containing the three perforated ulcers. Apparently, if my condition had been left untreated for much longer it would certainly have become life threatening.

Fortunately the operation was a success, but when my family rang the hospital to find out how the tests were progressing, one very angry consultant "played hell" with me when he found out I'd withheld the truth from them. His mood may have been somewhat exacerbated by the fact that two days after the operation he'd caught me wandering down a hospital corridor looking for the bathroom because I disliked intensely using the undignified bedside toilet facilities.

During and after my recovery the consultant, Mr de A'breu, and I became very firm friends and we were to spend many pleasant evenings together at the National Sporting Club boxing dinners at the Cafe Royal in London.

It was obvious, even for me to deduce, that the message my body was sending out loud and clear was slow down. The immediate need for major surgery made me reflect and examine my lifestyle to such an extent that I even contemplated retiring, but that reflective moment was shortlived and soon passed.

I did, however, acknowledge that I had to substantially reduce my workload and that decision is best illustrated by highlighting a very lucrative business opportunity which I turned down from a Liverpool based music agent around 1962.

I was having a social drink at the Coatham Hotel with some friends, including Rodger Barker and Ron Hall, when the receptionist informed me there was a telephone call from a music agent. As I answered, I recognised the apologetic, softly spoken, rather nervous tones of a young beat group manager. He asked me if he could cancel their performing contract for the following week because the group were about to make their first live appearance on a BBC television pop music programme. Given the circumstances and the career opportunity created by the nationwide exposure I didn't object to his request.

I was also impressed by his honesty and politeness because it had been known for bands and groups to fail to arrive at a venue without forwarding a reasonable explanation, so I was happy he'd at least taken the trouble to phone me in person.

The caller, with whom I was familiar, because I'd bought sheet music from his NEMS record store in Liverpool, was a genuine, hardworking and honest businessman and I wished him all the best for the television broadcast.

As we concluded our conversation he spoke glowingly about the Scouse group's potential and of his great belief that one day they would become very successful. He even asked me if I would consider buying a stake in the band. But I'd heard it all before. I'd had nearly 25 years experience of managers "talking up" the potential of their performers in order to obtain a booking. So I graciously declined the invitation, and besides, their style of deafening electric guitar music was not really to my taste. I still preferred the more cultured sound of the big band.

The name of the telephone caller to the Coatham Hotel that day was Brian Epstein. The group he was talking about was The Beatles and the rest, as they say, is history. Yeah, yeah, yeah.

Within a couple of years of that lunchtime conversation, electric guitar playing teenage groups would take over the venues once used by orchestras like mine and as the generation gap grew into a chasm, the era of the dance bands was drawing to a close.

In the early 1960s there was a major trend in showbusiness towards developing night clubs. The local establishments with names like Fiesta, Marimba and La Ronde married the performance of top quality cabaret artistes with restaurant and gambling facilities and business flourished during that "swinging" decade.

In response to the ever-increasing demand for nightlife I bought and refurbished two sites on Teesside, the old South Bank Empire Cinema and the administration block of Thornaby Aerodrome. The aerodrome site immediately took off (sorry) as a popular venue but it became a victim of its own success as objections to the noise of the late night revellers wending their weary way home became very vociferous. So, rather than become embroiled in protracted arguments with the local residents, I sold the building to the local Conservative Party.

During the conversion of the ageing cinema building it was suggested I should employ Wilf Mannion, who wished to return home from Ellesmere Port in Cheshire, as house manager. To have one of the greatest players in the history of Middlesbrough Football Club as part of the management team initially seemed to be a very appealing public relations exercise. But, although Wilf worked for us for about a year, the arrangement never quite reached its full potential and he eventually left by mutual agreement.

The South Bank Sporting Club quickly established itself on the "star circuit" and many of the top names of the day performed there, including Des O'Connor, with whom I enjoyed a Butlin reunion.

One of the most unusual evenings at the club occurred when a young singer, who had originally been billed as Gerry Dorsey, insisted on being introduced one night as Engelbert Humperdinck. I wasn't particularly bothered what he called himself as long as he fulfiled his contract. Despite the odd name he did sing rather well and went on to become one of the most popular ballad singers in the world with No.1 hits like Release Me, before eventually appearing in his own star-studded extravaganzas in the glitzy surroundings of Las Vegas.

The club was also used by Harold Wilson MP who had just been chosen as Leader of the Opposition following the sudden death of Hugh Gaitskill. He addressed a large gathering of the local Labour Party faithful to outline his own political vision. His speech must have been quite impressive because within a few months he was elected Prime Minister.

Although I enjoyed the entertainment side of the night club I was not very comfortable with the gaming aspect. I felt it was open to abuse, so after about four years I relinquished overall control of the South Bank Sporting Club to a well respected local retailer called Tony Heagney.

As I have previously outlined when recounting the fortuitous events surrounding my purchase of the Coatham Hotel in Redcar, it is often having the right contacts or even Lady Luck which can determine your next business venture. That was undoubtedly the case as I expanded my interest in the hotel trade throughout the 1960s and 1970s.

Nearly 40 years ago I became aware that draft plans were being discussed with regard to the construction of a major new arterial road linking the A19 to Teesside's expanding heavy industrial locations such as ICI Wilton and the Lackenby Steelworks to the south-east of Middlesbrough. In order to improve the infrastructure of the local area the proposed dual carriageway, which later became known as the Parkway, was to cut a swathe for over a mile through my land to the south of Normanby Hall.

At around the same time I had also renewed my acquaintance with Alf Finley, a local bookmaker and owner of the small Captain Cook Country Club on Stokesley Road in Marton, when my band played at his son's wedding in Middlesbrough Town Hall.

An observation worth making at this point is to reflect on the old saying: "Success Breeds Success". And while I'm not entirely convinced that's strictly true, there was a tendency on Teesside in the Sixties for the names of certain successful local people to become synonymous with business achievement. So, whenever any new land or property became available, their interest was always canvassed.

That was my experience with the Captain Cook Country Club in 1962 when I was informed, owing to personal reasons, that Alf Finley was willing to sell the property. With one eye on the location's long term feasibility I had no hesitation in meeting his offer for the premises.

The key determining factor when selecting any new site for possible development is its future potential. Being aware of the draft plans for the Parkway's preferred route, which included the construction of a large roundabout on the Stokesley Road adjacent to the Marton club, made the purchase of the property a very attractive proposition indeed. It also meant the Coatham Hotel, which was in need of a major modernisation, could be sold to the Scottish based Youngers Brewery and a strategy devised to concentrate on the full redevelopment of the Marton site.

The overall design and building of the new Marton complex was done solely by my own Parkway company. We even managed to retain the solid structure of the old house which had stood on the site, by incorporating it into the fabric of the new construction.

The modern hotel boasted 60 rooms, all with up to date en suite facilities and a ballroom which could cater for the largest of dinner dances. We also retained the club element of the complex, which had nearly 1,000 members. We renamed the whole development the Marton Hotel and Country Club.

The original plans for the Parkway roundabout were subsequently revised and we finally had to be content with having only slip lane access to the dual carriageway. That minor change, however, has not detracted from the overall success of the hotel which for the last 35 years has secured a very loyal clientele and established a fine reputation within the Teesside area and beyond for the all round quality of its accommodation, food, entertainment and conference facilities.

The Marton Hotel, under construction around 1964, with the original Captain Cook Country Club about to be amalgamated into the new building.

The impressive main ballroom of the Marton Hotel and Country Club in the 1960s.

An interesting innovation which those of you who have attended my dinner dances, particularly at the Marton Hotel, may not have been aware is the existence of our split level ballroom where the seating and table arrangements are on a slightly higher level than the main dance floor. The idea was developed as the result of the observations I made while playing with my band when we were on tour.

At certain times during the evening I'd noticed people enjoyed taking a short rest from the dancing. Unfortunately, during their break they didn't really become detached from the dance floor because they still remained on the same level as the dancers. In order to address that anomaly I decided to incorporate a raised tier around the floor space to provide a better vantage point from which to sit and watch. The concept proved very popular and created the effect of having two distinct and separate areas, one for dancing and another for relaxing and drinking, but both within the confines of the ballroom.

The idea became so successful that many venues up and down the country incorporated the layout into their establishments and some of the new premises even built balconies, a design feature which provided a marvellous viewing facility for onlookers.

The beauty of the countryside and coastline surrounding the Teesside conurbation, which we as residents take for granted, has always been a constant source of amazement for the first time visitor to our region, as the following interesting anecdote perfectly illustrates.

One Sunday morning in the 1960s I noticed a man standing alone in the lounge of the Marton Hotel waiting patiently for the bar to open. He appeared to be a little forlorn so I offered him an early drink, which he greatly appreciated. It transpired he was a journalist from a well known national newspaper whose brief was to write a story about the perceived harshness of living on industrial Teesside. In other words, another negative article endeavouring to denigrate our region.

I am proud to say I have lived in and around Middlesbrough all my life at a variety of addresses including Granville Road, Alexandra Road, Ash Grove, Flatts Lane, Ormesby Road and Normanby Hall and despite having had many job offers over the years to move south to London, I have always stayed in my native North-east.

But I do find it annoying when people, who have obviously never been to our area before, peddle the same monotonous stereotypical dour image of the region, and it was obvious, that the reporter had arrived with the same preconceived ideas. He did, however, make an encouraging start by changing his accommodation booking to the Marton Hotel when he saw the standard of our facilities.

As we chatted I told him I owned the hotel, and of my connection with Middlesbrough Football Club, and suggested if he required a conducted tour of the area I was more than willing to provide one.

The next few days proved to be a very illuminating and enlightening experience for our naive guest as I drove him through the idyllic North Yorks Moors and along the stunningly picturesque coastline. The sentence he constantly repeated had a very familiar ring to it: "I never knew this type of scenery existed in this part of the world."

During his stay he also sampled the warm local hospitality of a Neapolitan Evening, the excitement of a Boxing Night at the Marton Hotel and returned to his employer with a more realistic perspective of the diverse and attractive character of the Teesside area and its welcoming people.

The biased attitude of his newspaper was typical of the negative images which have long been perpetuated by the southern based media. It is a stigma with which our region, even today, seems to be unfortunately saddled.

My acquisition of the York Hotel site in Redcar followed a very similar pattern of events to that of the Marton development. I was approached by a trusted business associate with regard to the purchase of a large detached house on Coatham Road which was the base for a private members and folk club. I eventually acquired the property because, at that time, apart from the Coatham Hotel, Redcar had a distinct lack of venues with the necessary resources to cater for large social functions.

I'd previously tried to develop the catering facilities at the nearby Redcar racecourse but when in the middle of winter, frozen pipes caused the heating to fail and 200 frostbitten Prudential Insurance dinner guests had to be hurriedly transferred into the less salubrious surroundings of the main public bar area, my interest in developing the venue literally cooled.

Surrounding the folk club were other properties comprising of small cottages and various gardens rented by fishermen for the storage of their boats. Over a period of nine months, and without any pressure, I managed to acquire for the full market price most of the available housing stock. All the residents were given the opportunity to stay in their homes as tenants for as long as they required.

Eventually I owned enough land to undertake a total redevelopment of the site. I designed and built a compact hotel called the York, comprising of

50 modern en suite rooms and a licensed ballroom which could cater for around 400 people. Today the hotel is now called the Royal York in honour of the Duchess of Gloucester who officially re-opened the building in the 1970s after it was unfortunately badly damaged by fire, the cause of which was officially established as an electrical fault.

Over the years I believe all my hotels have built a solid reputation for providing the quality of service the people of Teesside demand and no doubt many of you will have attended a wide variety of functions at my establishments and I trust they were pleasurable experiences. Taking positive feedback as the yardstick, they must have been enjoyed, because even today at our hotels we have organisations and businesses willing to book three to five years in advance to make certain of specific dates for their annual dinner dances.

Reviewing the companies and organisations who have held their annual get togethers at either the Coatham, Marton or York hotels, it reads like a Who's Who of local businesses including: various ICI departments, numerous building firms, rugby clubs, the masons, the police, bookmakers, fish friers, insurance groups, Smith's Dock and Pickerings Lifts.

Our long-serving hotel managers, Ian Martin and Francisco de Sancho, both of whom have been with us for over 25 years.

It is obvious from the list that we have catered for a very wide cross-section of North-eastern society but I note that some of the organisations who began with me at the Coatham in the 1950s have ceased to exist, or as the economic climate of the area has changed they have either amalgamated with, or been taken over by, other firms and companies.

The sustaining of our lasting business reputation has been mainly due to the energetic directorship of my dedicated sons Kevan and Philip, but it is also a true reflection of the loyalty displayed by the staff, many of whom have been with us for years. I would especially like to mention the current hotel managers, Ian Martin and Francisco de Sancho, and our long serving "Queen Bee" Audrey. But to all our employees, both past and present, I must formally say I am extremely grateful for their enterprise, because without their conscientious endeavours over the last half a century, the hotels would not have been so commercially successful.

In October 1967 the introduction of the breathalyser dealt a temporary hammer blow to the financial viability of country pubs and restaurants. Many establishments experienced severe cash-flow difficulties as the legislation made an immediate impact on people's drinking and driving habits. Consequently the bar takings of the out of town premises plummetted.

At around that time the owner of the Tall Trees Hotel near Yarm was keen to sell his major shareholding in the property, so he could take up residence in the Isle of Man. I had previously entered into negotiations with regard to becoming a major shareholder in the business but those tentative talks had come to nothing. But it was not surprising when, in view of the prevailing volatile economic climate, I was again approached with regard to renewing my interest in the hotel. Fortunately for me it was a buyer's market and after some initial problems with stock valuation and the inherited accounts, I was finally able to acquire a large shareholding in the Tall Trees at a competitive and realistic price.

The Tall Trees was originally a large private house and had been turned into a hotel by the previous owner. Situated on the rural outskirts of Yarm and surrounded by 40 acres of its own grounds, there was certainly plenty of scope for redevelopment.

During our stewardship we supplemented the accommodation with 20 extra bedrooms, created a major water feature by adding a trout lake, built a ballroom for 200 people and added sporting facilities for golf, badminton and billiards.

Taking into account the effect of the breathalyser, the establishment traded very well for a number of years, considering it was a period when both the licensed industry and the general public were adapting to the new law by changing to non-alcoholic drinks or becoming dependant on taxis for their travel arrangements.

I eventually sold the Tall Trees Hotel in the 1980s to a progressive local businessman, Javed Ahmed, who has since successfully transformed the site into a massive entertainment centre with facilities specifically targeting the younger generation.

CHAPTER NINE

Ayresome Fully Aired

In 1963 I became involved with Middlesbrough Football Club, a team which I felt had been underachieving since its relegation from the First Division in Wilf Mannion's last season of 1954.

All through my life I've taken a keen interest in sport, particularly boxing and football. I played local league football on Teesside to a reasonable standard and once had a trial for Newcastle United. Unfortunately the serious injuries I sustained following my motorbike accident put paid to any further sporting aspirations I may have had, but I did fulfil some of my ambitions by firstly becoming a member and vice president of the National Sporting Club and then a director and chairman at Ayresome Park.

My initial involvement with the football club developed in the mid-1950s when I owned the Coatham Hotel. The Middlesbrough players of the period, Brian Clough, Alan Peacock, Ronnie Dicks, Peter Taylor etc, sometimes trained on Redcar beach and after their practice sessions they would often use the hotel's facilities to change and have some lunch. In order to foster a more positive link with the club I gave the players and officials complimentary tickets to any of my functions and occasionally organised club events for the manager Bob Dennison. Those arrangements proved to be sound public relations exercises as more often than not they were pictured in the local press.

At that time I'd been taking more than a passing interest in Teesside football's great underachievers who always promised a lot and delivered nothing. But my eventual active involvement was purely coincidental.

One morning, with the intention of buying a few shares in Middlesbrough

FC, I was perusing a shareholders list, which I'd acquired from Companies House, when I noticed the familiar name of a former pre-war insurance client who lived in Sycamore Road, Redcar, on the register. I contacted the particular lady in question to see if she wished to dispose of her ten shares and fortunately for me she was more than happy to do so.

When the club was originally formed during the Victorian era, 2,000 £1 shares were issued to raise the required capital. For some unknown reason, however, only around 1,600 of those shares were actually bought by investors.

My share purchase enabled me to attend the annual general meeting and question the directors about their total lack of ambition because nearly 40 years ago the club was in a desperate state of deep inertia and stagnation.

My conduct at the annual meetings could have been misconstrued as arrogant but I felt the club was going nowhere fast and the directors needed to be told that the Boro's loyal supporters were being very badly short changed by the board's lack of obvious endeavour.

It was during that period Middlesbrough FC had without doubt the best forward line in the Second Division with Brian Clough, who was scoring over 40 goals a season, being ably supported by Alan Peacock. Yet the team was struggling to gain promotion back to the top flight.

At one particular AGM I told the chairman, Mr WS Gibson, he was too much of a gentleman to run a football club and should resign. His response was typical of a gentleman because he thanked me sincerely for being so polite and promised he would make a note of my interest and suggestions.

My outspoken public criticism of the board, however, certainly struck a chord with some of Teesside's equally frustrated local businessmen and in early 1963 I was approached by Leslie French and Albert King with a view to mounting a possible takeover bid for the club.

Although I strongly agreed in principle with their general intentions, I wasn't too enamoured about becoming fully involved with the football club as I had just acquired the Marton Hotel and was fully committed to developing the site. It was, however, patently obvious that boardroom changes and the implementation of a radically different management structure were needed if the club was to improve its mediocre league standing.

So, armed with my register of the shareholders, we endeavoured to persuade a substantial percentage of those people listed to sell their holdings to us. It transpired that some were very willing to relinquish their interest but others would only give us their proxy votes. But at least my associates and I established that there was a definite groundswell of disgruntled support within the area against the board.

We also later received encouragement from Bob Dennison after he had been relieved of his managerial position in January 1963. He successfully sued the club for "unfair dismissal" and won substantial damages in the High Court. His willingness to be associated with the campaign for change certainly highlighted the deep rooted frustration that had built up even within the officers of the club.

However the directors of the football club got wind of our intentions and the chairman, Eric Thomas, who was a very pleasant and diplomatic local solicitor, requested an urgent meeting with me which we held at Normanby Hall.

Coming straight to the point, he asked me what our group wanted from the football club. I told him bluntly we wanted Leslie French and Albert King on the board. Mr Thomas told me that would not be possible because one of the directors, who I can only describe as a negative nuisance for the whole time he was on the board, for some reason disliked Leslie French. That news didn't surprise me because I'd crossed swords with him myself some years previously when as a representative of the local council he'd threatened to close down one of my dance halls in Stockton. After that altercation I never expected to deal with him again.

By April 1963 in an effort to solve the conflict of personalities a worried Eric Thomas devised a compromise which proposed that Albert King and myself joined the board in October 1963. We discussed the recommendation with Leslie French who thought it was a reasonable compromise, so we accepted the invitation.

I was however rather puzzled why we weren't immediately elected and had to wait another six months to become directors. But all was finally revealed when I read the club's Articles of Association. The board had required the breathing space in order to issue the balance of the unissued shares to ensure the club was kept firmly within their control.

When I eventually attended my first board meeting, Eric Thomas informed me that I'd also been allocated some new shares. I was asked if I had any initial comments to make. I hadn't, but I now knew the type of men I was dealing with. For the board to use such deliberate delaying tactics before allowing Albert and myself to take our seats confirmed to me just how close we were to gaining outright control of the club.

It didn't take me long to deduce that the only worthwhile revenue coming into the football club was through the turnstiles and via a minuscule amount of advertising. Not one director, and there were many wealthy individuals on the board, was willing to invest any of his own personal finance to give the club the capital injection it so badly needed. In fact the only financial commitment some of the board members had was the value of their own shares, which in few cases amounted to a paltry £20 investment.

In my early years as a director I soon realised I'd enrolled into an amiable old boys social club which met for a weekly chat and a sherry. If you also include the free travel to away games and the hospitality provided by other football clubs then it was a very pleasant way to spend your unambitious leisure time.

When I joined the board there were ten directors, far too many in my opinion to affect positive change within the club. They were too set in their ways and unfortunately the last thing on their minds appeared to be re-establishing Middlesbrough FC among football's elite, as the events of the early 1960s vividly highlight.

During my first couple of years as a board member I suggested many ideas for change but they were treated with guarded caution as I was the Johnny-Come-Lately who could easily be outvoted if necessary. I must note at this juncture that the admirable Jack Hatfield Snr, who unselfishly carried the club's sports equipment account for years, often sided with me at meetings. To have the support of such a highly regarded local businessman was something I very much appreciated because I'm sure he clearly understood my overall intentions and that I had the club's long-term interest at heart.

When, in February 1964, one of the club's prized assets, Alan Peacock, was sold to progressive Leeds United and replaced with players of inferior quality, my frustration increased as the stagnation deepened further. Peacock, like Brian Clough before him, was only reacting to the apathy at Ayresome Park and was tempted away to Elland Road by an offer from the ambitious Don Revie, and in the circumstances who could blame him.

Just prior to my association with Middlesbrough, the club had appointed a new manager in Raich Carter. He had been a player of great distinction and had built a successful promotion winning team at Leeds in the 1950s around the talented Welshman John Charles.

The relevant words to emphasise here are, had and been. Carter was without doubt an unmitigated disaster for the Boro. His appearances at training were infrequent, and in fact the organisation of those sessions seemed to be the sole responsibility of the hardworking and dedicated Harold Shepherdson. The standing joke at the time was that if you wanted to speak to the manager he could be found walking his dog along Redcar sands. However it was no laughing matter that the club was rapidly going downhill and gathering momentum. It was quite obvious to me Carter was not earning his money.

To make matters worse, he'd negotiated to be present at every board meeting. That arrangement gave him an unprecedented amount of power to affect the important decision making processes of the club. It was a situation I found unacceptable.

In February 1966, after we'd been unceremoniously thrashed at home by Huddersfield Town, and with the club's fortunes in freefall, I persuaded the chairman to call a crisis meeting of the senior directors at the York Hotel in Redcar.

During the focussed discussion it was unanimously decided that Raich Carter was not doing the job for which he was being paid. The only sensible course of action for us to take therefore, was to relieve him of his managerial responsibilities forthwith, and for the chairman to inform him of our deliberations the following day.

When I arrived at Ayresome Park the next morning at about 10:30 I had expected the meeting with the manager to have finished - but I was wrong. As I entered the ground I could hear a very angry raised voice emanating from the secretary's office, haranguing all and sundry. It was Raich Carter in a foul and very combative mood. When he saw me entering the offices he pointed his finger accusingly in my direction and shouted: " I blame you for this Amer. It's all your doing."

"You're probably right," I answered calmly, " but what you've done to this club is an absolute disgrace."

Obviously seething at my truthful candour, he replied with some sort of muttered veiled threat that one day he would sort me out, before leaving the ground as the ex-manager of Middlesbrough Football Club.

Unfortunately the belated sacking of Raich Carter could not save the Boro from their first ever relegation to the Third Division, but to be honest I'd seen it coming from the time I'd joined the board. It was a sad but inevitable conclusion to a period of gross apathy. The board were reaping the fruits of a decade that had lacked investment in both facilities and players.

Thankfully the club was given a fresh and rejuvenating impetus by two major factors. Firstly, hosting three games in the 1966 World Cup, and secondly, the inspired appointment of Stan Anderson as manager.

The World Cup really came to Middlesbrough by default because of a protracted dispute between Newcastle United and the City Council about ground modifications, which meant St James's Park could not stage any of their proposed group games. The matches were then offered to Middlesbrough, even though Ayresome Park had been previously overlooked by the FA, principally because of insufficient seating, very primitive sanitation arrangements and a complete lack of acceptable hospitality facilities.

At the initial board meeting to discuss the FA's formal approach, I told chairman Eric Thomas that in my professional opinion as a builder, Ayresome Park was in a state of total disrepair. The ground was suffering from years of neglect due to inadequate investment but the World Cup presented the club with a golden opportunity to upgrade the stadium, which should not be missed, particularly as the refurbishment was being underpinned with generous government grant provision.

In fact years before that terrible and tragic fire in the main wooden stand at Valley Parade, Bradford, in 1989, which claimed so many lives, I was very concerned, after receiving an informal ground insurance assessment, about the safety of Boro supporters, including me, who sat in the North Stand at Ayresome Park.

Situated below the original 1903 wooden construction was an antiquated coke and gas boiler house with its uncovered hot flue pipes running immediately under the seating. It was a potential disaster waiting to happen, but nothing was ever done to improve the facilities. One of my first priorities when I became chairman was to relocate the boiler house in a safe brick building away from the stands.

After an official FA visit to the ground, headed by Sports Minister Dennis Howell, it was eventually agreed Ayresome Park would host three group matches.

The proposed external changes to the ground were relatively straight forward. The Holgate End crowd barriers were reversed and strengthened, and fixed seating was installed in the north and south terraces and in the centre section of the partly roofed East End.

The internal changes behind the North Stand, which were to include new offices and function rooms to receive all the visiting dignitaries, proved to be much more problematic to complete.

At very short notice the builders, who had been engaged by the directors, informed the board they were unable to fulfil their contractual obligations. That unforseen circumstance created a situation which jeopardised the provision of the government grant. So, with time obviously pressing, I offered the club the services of my construction company, Parkway Estates, to continue with the upgrading work, even though at the time I was very busy transforming the Marton Hotel and Country Club and building some bungalows.

The work I undertook for Middlesbrough FC was done at cost price and I also provided all the extra labour required to make certain the project was finished on schedule. I had previously never carried out any building work at Ayresome Park, nor I must emphasise, had I sought to do so.

My prime motivation for volunteering to complete the renovations was to ensure the success of the World Cup on Teesside so that nobody, locally or nationally, could point a finger at the board and say Middlesbrough FC couldn't cope with the tournament organisation. The area's reputation was at stake and I felt duty bound to defend it.

My initial involvement with the refurbishment started badly, when it was established that the plans drawn up by the architect and quantity surveyor failed to identify that the proposed supports for the new Warwick Street building were in fact to be located directly over the main drains and sewers which served the ground. That oversight meant a great deal of unexpected remedial and bridging work had to be undertaken before the new structure could be erected in a safe and proper manner.

I was so furious at the ineptitude of the architect and surveyor that I persuaded the board to let me renegotiate their fees. My very firm stand led to protracted and often acrimonious discussions before a much lower charge was eventually agreed with those concerned.

Looking back, it was probably that incident which soured my relationship with fellow director Ernest Varley as he had been partly responsible for originally engaging the architects. For the next 20 years there was very seldom a board meeting which went by without some sort of caustic comment or verbal animosity taking place between Mr Varley and myself.

Completing the upgrading work was a race against time. We battled against persistent inclement winter weather, circumnavigated unidentified sewers, underpinned the main supports of the North Stand and totally renovated and redecorated the internal rooms. But against all the odds we were finally ready for the tournament with about a week to spare.

When the work was completed, Sports Minister Dennis Howell was given a conducted tour of the new facilities and he personally thanked me for my company's hard work. He was extremely impressed with the ground improvements which had been achieved in such a relatively short space of time. That was until he tried to view the alterations from the directors box in the North Stand. Turning towards me and speaking in a voice full of concern he said: "Charles, why are there no stairs up to the main stand?"

"Don't worry," I replied with a smile, "they're ready. They've been built in sections and will be fitted tomorrow. It's been done on purpose because I didn't want anybody climbing up to have a look around before we'd finished."

Parkway Estates incurred an operating loss in order to complete the work to my satisfaction. But considering the chaotic circumstances I'd inherited, I was very pleased with what had been achieved for Middlesbrough FC. Ayresome Park was ready for the World Cup and the club had a much improved stadium with which to greet our overseas guests.

The board was so impressed by the successful completion of the project on schedule that they decided that any future remedial work at Ayresome Park should be carried out by Parkway Estates or overseen by me if specialist outside contractors were required. I must emphasise again, I did not seek the informal agreement and I only accepted the offer on the insistance of the directors.

The understanding stayed in place until I resigned as chairman in 1982, with one exception when the main dressing rooms were renovated by a firm engaged by a fellow director with disastrous results. The original estimates were exceeded and condensation damage caused rising damp and the paint to peel off the walls. The remedial work needed to rectify the shoddy standard of workmanship meant the club effectively paid twice for the same contract. It was money wasted, and I ensured it never happened again.

Although the attendances at Ayresome Park during the 1966 World Cup were rather disappointing, largely due to the high ticket costs imposed by FIFA and the misguided perception that a group containing Italy, USSR, Chile and North Korea was uninspiring, we did witness one of the biggest upsets of that or any World Cup when the unfancied North Koreans defeated the mighty Italians.

The North Korean team played all their matches at Ayresome Park and during the early stages of the tournament the squad stayed at the Marton Hotel and Country Club. They were a wonderful, happy and courteous delegation who were not used to the comfortable accommodation and service they were accorded.

The Teesside public instantly took the diminutive players to their hearts and that support was much appreciated by the North Korean team and their management.

I remember one particular night when Middlesbrough FC hosted a dinner in their honour at the Marton Hotel. I was sitting adjacent to the top table near Boro chairman Eric Thomas and the North Korean Sports Minister. As the red house wine was brought round by the waiters I noticed the Sports Minister, who had apparently been a proficient wrestler and was of a size with which you didn't argue, look accusingly at his glass. Through the interpreter I enquired if there was a problem with the drink.

"Not really," came the reply, "But would it be possible for the minister to have a Drambuie instead?"

Complying with the request was of course not a problem, but during the next couple of hours the minister proceeded to polish off a bottle and a half of Drambuie on his own and then he amazingly asked for another to take to bed. Now that's what I call drinking in any language. To cap it all, he was one of the first to rise for breakfast early the following morning.

On another occasion I invited the whole delegation to be my guests at Normanby Hall but unfortunately, due to business commitments, I forgot about their time of arrival and when my wife answered a knock at the front door she was greeted by the smiling faces of the North Korean football team and officials expecting to attend an informal function. After a few frantic family telephone calls to contact me I hastily returned home to find Margaret, as usual, coping very well with our guests who appeared quite content drinking coffee and whisky despite the temporary absence of their embarrassed host.

What struck me most forcibly about that visit was the look of wonderment on the their faces as they walked around the spacious house and grounds of the hall. Their reaction made me reflect on what life must have been like for them in their austere communist country. We often grumble about conditions in Britain but at least we live in a relatively free democratic society unlike our Asian visitors at that time. As a token of our appreciation, I gave them all a Churchill crown to commemorate their visit to Middlesbrough.

The North Koreans were so impressed with our hospitality towards them during the World Cup tournament that I was constantly invited to visit their country and observe at first hand the new sports complexes they were building. Judging from the brochures I received the proposed developments were state of the art facilities, much more advanced than anything we were undertaking in this country during the 1960s. I was very flattered with the invitations and their appreciative reaction totally vindicated the choice of Middlesbrough as a World Cup venue.

Our intensive preparation for the World Cup had certainly been hectic but our stage of the tournament was without doubt a total success. What a shame that Middlesbrough would begin the new season in the Third Division for the first time in their history.

In the spring of 1966 the appointment of Stan Anderson as manager of Middlesbrough, which was proposed by George Kitching, was an uncharacteristic masterstroke by the board.

He had been signed as an experienced player from Newcastle United the previous year, after negotiations between their chairman Lord Westwood and Boro director Mr. Kitching. Despite being made team captain he was, however, unable to prevent the embarrassment of being relegated to the Third Division.

Immediately after Anderson's appointment as manager, the atmosphere in the dressing room changed dramatically. Gone was the rather acrimonious undercurrent which had greatly affected team spirit, with veiled suggestions that certain players were deliberately not trying, to be replaced with an air of confident, optimistic determination.

Stan was one of the most pleasant men I have ever met in football. A real gentleman. He revitalised the club by winning promotion in his first season and making some very astute signings, often on the advice and recommendation of George Kitching, including that great Boro favourite John Hickton along with John O'Rourke, Stuart Boam, John Craggs and Graeme Souness.

Anderson also encouraged the young talents of Willie Maddren, David Mills and David Armstrong to blossom and without a shadow of a doubt I can say it was Stan who laid the solid foundations on which Jack Charlton's managerial success in the middle 1970s was built.

Stan's only fault was that he was not forceful enough, particularly when dealing with the directors. Confrontation was not part of his character. He was often almost apologetic when it came to asking for the money to finance transfers. I became so frustrated with him after one particular board meeting that I took him to one side and told him if he ever wanted money to strengthen the team I'd personally back his judgement. I think he appreciated my interest and advice.

Stan Anderson turned Middlesbrough Football Club around in the late 60s and early 70s. The Boro were constantly among the front runners for promotion to the First Division and twice reached the FA Cup quarter finals under his stewardship. However his inability to regain Middlesbrough's top flight status became a constant source of frustration and a millstone round his neck and Stan eventually resigned in the spring of 1973 believing he could do no more for the club. In hindsight he was probably right, but I feel he played a very important part in the resurgence of the Boro as a real footballing force and his sterling endeavours should be formally recognised.

I must state honestly from the outset of this next section, that I was totally against Jack Charlton becoming manager of Middlesbrough in May 1973. I felt we should have appointed somebody of greater managerial experience, but fortunately I was outvoted and the rest of the story, as they say, is history. I am pleased to acknowledge that Jack went on to become one of Middlesbrough's most successful managers of all time.

Jack's appointment almost coincided with my own as chairman of Middlesbrough. The incumbent was George Whinney who had been on the board for 23 years, but he'd only been chairman for about 12 months. He was the head of a family timber importing firm based in Hartlepool but because of business pressure and the need to make frequent trips to Canada, he'd stood down both as chairman and as a director of the club. He was replaced on the board by Michael McCullagh who had acquired the shares of former director Albert King when he had unfortunately passed away.

I had no indication at the time, but the actions of McCullagh over the next 12 years were to have a major impact on my personal life and of course, as a future chairman, he was in the thick of Middlesbrough Football Club's battle for its very existence.

I first met Michael McCullagh in the early 1970s at a Marton Hotel social function. He stopped me in the foyer and, after introducing himself, he bluntly asked me whether it was true that my agreement was required before any new members were elected to the board of Middlesbrough Football Club. I was quite surprised by his forthright manner because I'd no idea who he was and I politely told him he'd been totally misinformed. In reality it was most unlikely that my single vote would have influenced the election of any proposed new board member.

Once he'd joined the board, to which I wish to emphasise I raised no objections, I found him to be a keen and willing director. I gladly gave him advice regarding the vagaries of planning applications for his developing business, the Marske Machine Company, and I also helped him to resolve a problem with the education of one of his children. I even extracated him from his damaged vehicle and made sure he was taken to hospital when he was injured in a car accident near Yarm. But I was not prepared for what I regarded as his vindictive attitude towards me when, under his unsuccessful chairmanship, I felt that convenient scapegoats were being sought in order to deflect criticism away from the club's dire financial plight from 1983-85.

My unanimous appointment as chairman of the board was a total surprise. I did not actively seek the position, nor did I think I merited it. I felt there were other longer serving directors who were much more deserving of the prestigious position than me.

Although I had to be persuaded to accept the post I was an extremely proud man when I became the chairman of Middlesbrough Football Club. From the outset it was my ambition to fulfil the dormant potential of my hometown club and I can honestly state, without fear of any contradiction, that every decision I made during my tenure in control was always done with the best interests of the club and its long suffering, success starved, supporters at heart.

One of my first tasks at the helm was to have a private meeting with Jack Charlton and his wife Pat, to impress upon him that although I had not initially approved of his appointment, he could now rely on my fullest support and as the new manager of Middlesbrough he would be given total control over all team affairs, with no boardroom interference whatsoever.

I felt he appreciated my candour and we both knew where we stood, right from the start of our relationship, which was vital if the football club was to progress in the way I envisaged.

Jack made it quite clear soon after his appointment that he intended to work without a formal contract and, all being well, he would probably stay with Middlesbrough for about four seasons. As it turned out he was true to his word. Since stepping down in April 1977, however, he has gone on the record numerous times to say that in hindsight he left the Boro with only half the job completed. He believed if he'd stayed longer then a major trophy could have been brought to Ayresome Park.

I certainly concur with that assessment because I also felt he moved on far too quickly, although I did detect in his final season that the dressing room was not as united as it had been in previous years. In particular Terry Cooper, who had been bought from Charlton's old club Leeds United, often seemed to me to be at the heart of the unrest. Perhaps Jack could see the writing on the wall and as with most things in life, timing is everything.

A proud moment as I'm formally presented with the Second Division Championship Trophy for 1973-74 by Len Shipman, the president of the Football League, on the pitch at Ayresome Park.

Members of the promotion winning side of 1973/74, proudly display the Second Division Championship Trophy.

Structural engineer George Gowland and myself admire the view from the new television gantry, instigated by Jack Charlton, and erected at Ayresome Park to coincide with the club's return to the First Division in 1974.

*Good times. Jack Charlton and Charles Amer.
A very successful partnership.*

Jack Charlton was and still is his own man, uncomplicated, forthright, down to earth, with no frills. You take him as you find him and it was obvious, when we had a meeting to discuss his public decision to leave, that he would not be persuaded to change his mind, so it was pointless even to try. The board had to regrettably accept that it was looking for a new manager.

I must admit I was personally very disappointed with Jack's decision because I felt as long as he was in charge of Middlesbrough Football Club we were a force to be reckoned with in the First Division. We were a team that no other club, including the Liverpools of this world, relished playing. But when Jack left, so did the feeling of security.

After Jack's departure the manager's job was initially offered to Harold Shepherdson but he gracefully declined the invitation. Harold was always at his happiest working studiously behind the scenes away from the limelight.

Jack Charlton was the total antithesis of Stan Anderson both in personality and demeanour. He was an extrovert manager who wore his heart on his sleeve. He knew exactly how he wanted his team to play and the team eventually became an extension of his character, well organised, determined and difficult to beat.

He did, however, in his record breaking Second Division championship winning first season of 1973/74, make one signing which I feel certainly changed the whole course of his early managerial career. That was the very astute signing of Bobby Murdoch from Celtic, and I can vividly recall the events surrounding the transfer.

I was sitting in the lounge of Normanby Hall reading the Evening Gazette early one Friday evening when I saw Jack Charlton's Range Rover come roaring up the drive. As he hurriedly made his way to the rear entrance of the hall, I deduced from his body language that he seemed to be in a mild panic.

It transpired he'd just received a call from Celtic manager Jock Stein informing him that ex-Scottish international Bobby Murdoch was available on a free transfer and he could have first refusal. I've never before or since seen Jack so enthusiastic about the possibility of signing a player. After a brief chat to reassure him I didn't need to convene a formal board meeting in order to sanction the transfer, we clarified some of the financial details between ourselves and signed Bobby Murdoch that evening over the telephone from my house.

The reasons for Jack's unbridled enthusiasm were twofold. Not only was he acquiring a player of proven quality but he also saw the vastly experienced Murdoch as the person to harness the untapped potential of the talented, if wayward young Scot, Graeme Souness.

As the 1973/74 season progressed with crowds in excess of 25,000 finally filling Ayresome Park, it became abundantly clear why Jack Charlton was so keen to buy Bobby Murdoch. Here was the vital missing piece of the jigsaw which had so cruelly eluded Stan Anderson for at least five years and it had been handed to Jack Charlton on a plate. Both he and Middlesbrough FC were eternally grateful as we won promotion to the First Division in a canter by a record 15 points from our nearest rivals Luton Town.

The club certainly benefited from having such a high profile manager as Jack Charlton and one example of his notoriety that comes readily to mind was on our tour of Australasia in the summer of 1975. Jack was feted wherever we went. He even played in some of the exhibition matches, as I recall, scoring the odd goal into the bargain. It was certainly a gratifying time in the club's history.

My lasting memory of the trip occurred on the idyllic island of Tahiti where we were treated like royalty. As club chairman you often have to attend formal functions and meet the dignitaries of the host club or nation without the players, who are left to relax and top-up their tans by the hotel pool.

One particular afternoon George Kitching and myself were invited to the residence of the mayor of the Tahitian capital Papeete. While we were being escorted around the tropical hot houses of his thriving orchid growing business, I was introduced to a youth who was wearing a football kit. It transpired he was the grandson of the mayor and had been selected as a substitute for the Tahitian Select XI to play against Middlesbrough the same evening in a friendly match.

The mayor explained to me how much his grandson wanted to be footballer and that the match against Middlesbrough provided a big opportunity for him to fulfil his ambition, especially as representatives of the Tahitian FA were attending the match looking for prospective talent.

I must admit I was very puzzled as to where the conversation was leading, until he asked if it was possible for me to persuade Mr Jack Charlton to allow his grandson to score a goal against Middlesbrough to increase his chances of impressing the Tahitian officials. I almost choked on my lager at his request and replied: "Mr Mayor, if you can convince Jack Charlton to allow somebody to deliberately score a goal against his team, even in an exhibition match, I'll retire now. I can assure you it just won't happen."

As I left the mayor's residence I had to smile at his audacity but then I thought of Jack's bluff reaction and my smile soon evaporated. For the record we won the match easily 6-0 with Jack coming on as a substitute to score one of the goals.

Jack Charlton's management career at Middlesbrough was an undoubted success with guaranteed First Division stability, an FA Cup quarter-final and a League Cup semi-final, but I always felt we were one or two players short of being a first class side. We needed a top class goalscorer to replace John Hickton and in my opinion Jack was indecisive in the transfer market, preferring to look for short term bargains like Alf Wood, rather than investing for the future in younger talent.

Contrary to the popular opinion at the time, money was always available for the acquisition of new players. The board cannot and should not be held responsible for Jack's frugal and often tentative dealings in the transfer market.

A prime example of Jack's hesitancy surrounded the transfer of the big, bustling Burnley striker Ray Hankin who we were prepared to buy for a fee of around £180,000. After I had agreed to the deal, Jack had second thoughts and while he was dithering, Hankin signed for Leeds United.

Although Jack meant well and his heart was in the right place he occasionally caused the board problems because he would insist on making unilateral decisions that affected the club without consulting the directors. He often thought that Middlesbrough was his club and that he was in overall control of the decision making process. That was not the case. A football club is ultimately the responsibility of the board and the example of the proposed development of the South Stand executive boxes will highlight the point I'm trying to make.

In the mid-1970s with the Boro firmly established in the First Division, there were many discussions at boardroom level on how to upgrade Ayresome Park into a premier sports stadium. One tentative suggestion was to move the ground's location. Another idea was to increase the club's revenue by building some executive boxes which could be used for corporate hospitality, but the siting of the boxes within the stadium proved to be problematic.

In 1976 Jack Charlton and a colleague Mac Murray, working I have no doubt with the club's best interest at heart, commissioned some detailed drawings of a number of executive boxes to be situated at the rear of the South Stand terracing and presented them to the board.

Comprehensive local press coverage was given to the proposed new innovation and a reception organised to formally launch the project. I must admit I was initially very impressed when I saw the planned facilities for the first time. They looked excellent and I told Jack so.

I intuitively sensed that something was wrong, however, when I enquired who had taken the formal sightlines for the development and how many season ticket holders would have their view of the pitch obscured by the elevated nature of the hospitality boxes. My enquiry was met with a stoney silence. I was informed that nobody had in fact taken any sightlines prior to the completion of the drawings and therefore they were unable to tell me how it would effect the spectators who sat in the South Stand.

Amazed at such an elementary architectural mistake, I later went to the South Stand myself armed with the drawings and a building foreman from Parkway Estates. After some precise mathematical calculations we established the proposed height of the boxes and discovered that 800 seated spectators, including 350 season ticket holders, would be unable to see at least a quarter of the pitch.

The financial cost of losing that amount of seating plus over 2,200 standing places on the terrace meant the scheme was not commercially viable and so it was shelved.

Jack was extremely disappointed when he realised the development was flawed. It gave me no pleasure at all in highlighting its shortcomings, because in principle it had my full support as I was keen to increase both the club's revenue and profile. If only proper consultations in the pre-planning stage had been undertaken at boardroom level I could have quite quickly pointed out the pitfalls and saved Jack the embarrassment. But that was typical Jack, get an idea and jump in with two feet before you have fully investigated the consequences.

Ayresome Park was constantly upgraded during the 1970s to meet the standards required by the FA and the Safety of Sports Ground legislation. One of the most pressing areas of the ground to receive attention was the very primitive open air toilet facilities between the South Stand and the East End which amounted to little more than tin sheeting leaning against the surrounding wooden fence.

Once the modern toilet facility had been provided I was amazed to receive a complaint about the new enclosed urinals from an elderly local resident. Pursuing the complaint personally, it transpired the lady in question was very annoyed with me because the gents was no longer visible from her upstairs window and I had in fact spoilt her half-time entertainment. How do you even begin to answer a complaint like that?

When I was appointed chairman one of the first decisions I took was to acknowledge the contributions made to Middlesbrough FC by secretary Harry Green and Harold Shepherdson by substantially raising their wages, because over the years they were two of the club's most loyal servants.

I also wish to formally record that, in my opinion, their treatment by the club, after I'd resigned the chair in 1982, was a heartless act of insensitivity. The actions of certain board members who were driven by their overriding desire to cut the club's spiralling weekly debts was despicable. I was so angry when I saw the proposals that Harry and Harold were being asked to take a cut of 50 per cent in their wages, that Kevan and I walked out of the board meeting in disgust.

Club secretary Harry Green and I view the exhibits on display during an open day held at Ayresome Park, attended by thousands of Middlesbrough supporters.

Harry Green was the club's secretary for nearly 20 years. He was one of the most honest, trustworthy and hardworking men I have ever met in my entire life. During my chairmanship he was so financially meticulous he would always be pestering me to check his petty cash book. He was extremely conscientious and worked tirelessly for the good of Middlesbrough, so much so that his health sometimes suffered. The club's bills were always paid on time and Harry became so well respected within the game that on many occasions officials from other clubs, much more famous than ours, would ask for his considered opinion on matters relating to football administration. The Boro owe him a great debt of gratitude but the manner of his low profile retirement in October 1982 did little to enhance the reputations of some of the directors at that time.

Harold Shepherdson's contribution to Middlesbrough FC was immeasurable. He served the club in a variety of capacities for over 45 years and often took the managerial helm in times of crisis. He was a marvellous unassuming and distinguished ambassador for the club and I never heard him say a wrong word about anybody. He was well liked and respected throughout the whole football world.

When he became England trainer in the 1950s it was an appointment of which the club should have been justly proud. But curiously enough when I joined the board in 1963 I detected an envious undercurrent towards him from certain directors. Why that state of affairs had developed was beyond me. Here was an official of Middlesbrough FC elevated to one the country's most prestigious football positions in the land and he was not even receiving the credit he deserved from within his own club. I believe that the lack of recognition was rooted in the petty jealousy of Harold's achievements. There was even a bizarre suggestion at a board meeting by one director that the income he received from his England duties should be deducted from his basic Middlesbrough salary. To my mind that was an outrageous remark and it was quite rightly never taken seriously. The free publicity and kudos the club received when Harold Shepherdson was the England trainer far outweighed any extra income he earned. In my opinion he deserved every penny, as it was a true reflection of his status within the game. He was a prized asset which some Middlesbrough directors unfortunately failed to recognise.

An example of the numerous innovations suggested by Harold, and one which was copied by other clubs, was the acquisition of an apprentices hostel. Situated in The Avenue, Middlesbrough, the facility provided young lads, who were often away from home for the first time, with a stable environment in which to stay. I have no doubt it enabled them to settle more quickly into the area rather than being in solitary digs. I thought the whole concept was a marvellous idea and I personally agreed to fund Harold's judgement when a prompt decision was needed to acquire the property for the club, prior to the board's formal ratification.

In 1982 Harold was executive officer in charge of football, but like Harry Green he became a statistic in a cruel cost cutting exercise. I know for a fact that Shep was deeply hurt by his shabby treatment and although his public relations skills were belatedly utilised again by the Boro's new regime, in my opinion it was too little too late because the damage to Harold's pride had already been done. When he died, in September 1995, I am still convinced he bore the scars of that personal insult. He was a proud man who had given nearly all his working life to his local town football club and although naming the access road leading to the new Riverside Stadium, Shepherdson Way, was a thoughtful if belated gesture, I'm afraid it only partly compensates for the unnecessary unpleasantness Harold had to endure from certain insensitive officers of the club he loved.

As the chairman of a football club you often have to deal with players who are unsettled and one of the strangest transfer requests I ever received came from the 1970s cult hero Alan Foggon while we were on a club tour of New Zealand.

Prior to playing their national team we were staying at a very pleasant hotel on the South Island near Christchurch and to reach our well appointed chalet accommodation, we had to walk through some beautiful ornamental gardens. One warm evening George Kitching and I were returning to our rooms, after a convivial function in the lounge, when suddenly a shadowy figure darted out of the undergrowth and thrust an envelope into my hand. Before I could fully comprehend what was happening, he was gone.

Back in my room I discovered the envelope contained a written transfer request from striker Alan Foggon. The following morning I informed the other board members in the tour party of the previous night's bizarre event, and we quickly decided to grant the request.

Cliff Mitchell of the Evening Gazette was covering the tour for the readers back home, so I notified him with regard to the Foggon situation and the red hot transfer news was immediately dispatched across the world in time for the evening editions.

I think Foggon, who could be slightly surly at times, was rather taken aback by the indecent haste of our decision and if my memory serves me well, it wasn't long after we returned to Middlesbrough that the request was withdrawn.

Graeme Souness was undoubtedly a prodigious footballing talent, a marvellous passer of the ball and tough competitor. When he was signed from Spurs in 1972, we were warned by their canny manager Bill Nicholson that he needed to be controlled with a firm hand and so it turned out.

On his own admission, when Souness arrived at Ayresome Park he was overweight, flash, fancied himself and displayed more than a passing interest in the opposite sex. Modesty was also a word alien to his vocabulary.

However, under the managerial guidance of Jack Charlton and the playing guile of Bobby Murdoch, Souness became one of the most gifted and influential midfield players in the country. Some would argue he was Middlesbrough's greatest player of all time, capped by Scotland and constantly watched by other leading clubs. Off the pitch, it's true that he was a bit of a handful and a socialite. He enjoyed frequenting the local night clubs and driving fast cars. But on match days it has to be said Graeme was always totally committed to Middlesbrough Football Club.

While Jack was at the helm Souness played as well as anybody in a red shirt, but in the spring of 1977 when Jack stepped down and the club was managerless and in a state of limbo I felt that Souness, who was due to sign a new contract, tried to exploit the situation. He made excessive tax free financial demands which the club could not afford, and in order to preserve dressing room harmony, I certainly would not meet. Whether he was holding out to see who was appointed as the next manager or possibly in his own mind he had already decided to leave Ayresome Park I don't know, but by the time we left for a pre-arranged tour of Australasia he still had not re-signed. In fact Harry Green took the relevant paperwork with him on tour.

In order to fulfil the official part of the tour itinerary I accompanied the coaching staff abroad and left vice-chairman George Kitching to interview John Neal, who was a candidate for the vacant manager's position, and had been highly recommended to us by the respected Newcastle chairman Lord Westwood.

The first leg of our tour took us to Hong Kong where we arrived nearly two days late after our plane had been grounded by engine trouble in the Indian city of Bombay. The delay gave the players an unexpected chance to prove themselves more than adept at diplomacy and public relations by helping the elderly and young children who were also on the flight. I felt that their conduct during a very frustrating 48 hours wait did much to enhance the reputation of the club.

Despite their obvious tiredness the team played two exhibition matches in Hong Kong but when we assembled at the airport to fly on to Australia there was no sign of Souness and the flight took off without him. He eventually arrived two days later with no valid explanation for his absence and I never pursued the matter. On reflection he should really have been disciplined and sent home but that severity of punishment would have only made unwelcome headlines in the tabloids back home.

Once he was in Australia, Souness was approached by several local clubs with requests to make guest appearances for them once we had completed the tour.

When he asked for permission to extend his stay, he was informed that it would not be a problem, as long as he had signed his new contract.

When John Neal was appointed as our new manager I insisted that he flew out to Australia to meet the players and officials. It has to be acknowledged that Neal had done a very sound job on limited resources at Third Division Wrexham. But with the benefit of hindsight his appointment was a misjudgement that probably wouldn't have occurred if I'd been in England. His manner and general approach were far too low key and he did not convey any of Jack Charlton's enthusiasm for the job either to the players or the supporters.

On his arrival I informed him about the Graeme Souness situation and he asked if he could continue with the negotiations. I did warn him that under no circumstances was Souness to stay in Australia without re-signing.

Although he was initially keen to conduct the contract talks it quickly became obvious that Neal seemed unable to cope with Souness. During one meeting in my hotel room he tried to assure me that Souness would definitely sign his contract once he got home. I must admit my reply was rather curt when I heard his plea bargain on behalf of the player. I told Neal that there was no difference between Souness signing his contract in Australia than at home, and I emphasised the point that if he didn't re-sign he would be returning to England with the rest of the tour party.

Neal must have relayed my terse feelings to the player because a few days later Souness knocked on my door, almost apologetically, asking to speak to me about his offers of guest appearances.

By now I was fast becoming very frustrated with the whole saga, so I took him on to the balcony, out of earshot of my wife, and explained in no uncertain terms, interspersed with a few choice expletives, that the club's position was crystal clear. Unless he signed his contract before I left for home, to deal with some urgent business commitments, he would not be staying in Australia and with that explanation ringing in his ears, he left the room.

The day before my departure, representatives of the Australian FA kindly organised an official "goodbye" lunch at the famous revolving tower restaurant in Sydney. During the meal I was informed that a Mr Souness wanted to see me as a matter of urgency. Not wishing to leave our hosts I asked Harry Green to deal with the request. A short while later he returned with the contract formalities complete.

By re-signing, Souness was able to stay in Australia for a very lucrative six weeks. But having forced his hand, I wondered whether we had only postponed his inevitable departure.

Early in the 1977/78 season Souness was very unsettled and became a negative influence in the dressing room. Speculation was rife in the media about his imminent departure from Ayresome Park. During that period there was a suspicion in my mind that Graeme Souness was consciously underachieving and the supporters were being short-changed by one of their star players. It was a situation which caused me grave concern.

It was also patently apparent that John Neal found him difficult to deal with and he was becoming increasingly ineffectual in most of the matches he played. The final straw came with the symbolic removal of his shirt when he was substituted on the last day of 1977 at Ayresome Park against Norwich City. That gesture angered me so much that I immediately phoned John Smith, the chairman of Liverpool, to set up a meeting in a Leeds hotel to discuss Souness's transfer. He had very publicly declared his negative feelings towards Middlesbrough FC and I had come to the conclusion, the quicker he was transferred the better.

Although there were many clubs interested in signing Souness I contacted John Smith because I knew he was a gentleman and had the reputation of being very fair with regard to transfer negotiations. He was above all a person I knew I could trust. We had come to know each other quite well because we sat together at the league chairman's meetings and found, among other things, we had a mutual interest in Bechstein pianos.

Our personal discussions in the hotel lounge, which were very businesslike, didn't last long and we settled on a realistic transfer figure of £325,000. Although the Liverpool manager Bob Paisley was initially taken aback by the size of the fee I have no doubts that the deal proved to be a sound piece of business for both clubs.

Graeme Souness went on to become one of Liverpool's greatest post war players, winning numerous trophies and captaining both his club and country. But I certainly feel he owes Middlesbrough FC and particularly Stan Anderson and Jack Charlton a great debt of gratitude for resurrecting his football career. But I'm afraid I'll never forget the manner of his undignified departure from Ayresome Park.

Speaking of debts, he still owes me money for a personal loan obtained for him through my company in 1977 to buy a new car. The terms of the agreement were that he would repay the money through weekly instalments. I never saw a penny. We even wrote him letters after his transfer, addressed to Liverpool Football Club, which he failed to acknowledge.

Up to the beginning of the 1997/98 season Middlesbrough have never won a major football trophy in their 121 year history. During my tenure as chairman we did succeed in securing the unfashionable Anglo-Scottish Cup in December 1976 and the Japan Cup in the summer of 1980. The latter was quite a prestigious invitational tournament played against the Japanese and Chinese national teams, Espanol from Spain and a young Argentine select side which included Diego Maradona. We competed well and were unbeaten during the whole competition and fully merited our success.

While we were in Japan I must admit I was very impressed by the meticulous organisation of Japanese society and in particular the famous "bullet train".

On one occasion our party was standing at a station waiting for the train's arrival when I noticed some brilliant white dots marked on the edge of the platform. I asked our tour guide what they were for and he told me that when the train pulled into the station the carriage doors must open adjacent to those marks. I was rather sceptical about the explanation but my doubts were soon dispelled when the train arrived, not only precisely on schedule, but it came to a standstill exactly opposite the aforementioned white marks. Very impressive indeed.

Another lasting memory I have of Japanese society was how they utilised every inch of available land. No open space was wasted. That convention was perfectly illustrated when we visited a golf driving range, which was about four storeys high and housed hundreds of robotic golfers purposefully striking balls into the sky with no fairway or green in sight. With land at such a premium, I wonder if any of those would-be professionals ever actually graduated to playing on a real course.

In my lifetime Middlesbrough FC have always been accused of selling their playing assets but as chairman I can honestly say I never deliberately sold a player.

Now that may appear to be somewhat of a contradictory statement to make in the light of certain events but I want to emphasise at this point, while I have the opportunity, that all the players who left Middlesbrough during my chairmanship did so of their own accord. None of them had to be transferred. The hard truth of the matter was that neither the manager nor the board of directors could stop any player who was determined to try and better himself elsewhere and was adamant about leaving.

Once in a while, however, an offer for a player came along which was so tempting it was impossible to turn down but even in those circumstances the player concerned had to agree to the move. That was the case with the sale of David Mills in January 1979.

David had been a fine and loyal Middlesbrough player for nearly ten years. The club had recognised his talent as a youngster when he played for Arthur Head School and Stockton and Billingham Boys. We even retained him when, as a youngster, he developed a serious back problem which kept him out of football for over a year.

The chairman of West Bromich Albion, Bert Millichip, enquired about David's availability and confirmed that his manager, Ron Atkinson, was keen to sign the player and asked us to name our price. I spoke to my fellow director George Kitching about the approach and we decided that it wasn't in the best interests of the club to sell such a conscientious player as David, so we'd ask for the highly inflated price of half a million pounds, which at that time would have been a record transfer between two English clubs.

The asking price was duly relayed back to West Brom and we honestly thought that would be an end to their enquiry. But to our complete surprise West Brom agreed the transfer fee with very little further negotiation and David Mills was sold.

From Middlesbrough's point of view it was a very sound piece of business and because he hadn't formally asked for a move the financial rewards for David were very attractive indeed.

The transfer entered the record books for a short while and, although it has to be said he never performed as consistently with any other club once he'd left Ayresome Park, in January 1979 David Mills' transfer came at the right time for all the parties concerned and I personally never regretted the deal.

At the request of Council Leader Charles Shopland, I visited the children of Whinney Banks Primary School to talk about the club's tour of Japan in 1980.

As I have stated previously, all the directors of Middlesbrough FC, with the notable exception of Jack Hatfield Jnr, were loathe to commit any personal finance to the club. The disagreement surrounding the signing of Darren Wood as a full-time professional, in July 1981, perfectly highlights the situation which existed.

Wood was a highly promising apprentice who wanted an advance on his signing on fee to invest in his father's business. In principle the board had no objection to the club advancing him the money but Harry Green was advised that under FA rules the procedure would not be possible. When I proposed the board should try and help the lad out with the directors "chipping in" some money from their own pockets, it was rejected. So much for the caring face of football.

In the end Jack Hatfield Jnr and myself put together a personal financial package that didn't involve any club monies, but which still enabled us to sign Darren Wood for Middlesbrough FC.

That episode was yet another example of the unwillingness of certain directors to display some financial commitment to the club and guarantee that home-produced young talent stayed at Ayresome Park.

Just after I'd resigned as chairman in 1982 Liverpool made a positive enquiry about teenager Wood and offered around £250,000 for his signature. That bid was rejected but it highlighted the keen interest the larger clubs were taking in his development.

As the crisis at Middlesbrough worsened during 1983/84, the board was forced to pursue other avenues of raising capital and the short-lived Boro Bonanza Society was created. The only marketable playing asset at that time was Darren Wood, who had performed consistently well in a poor team. But because of their dire cash-flow situation the club were not in a strong bargaining position when Chelsea and ex-Boro manager John Neal offered a part exchange deal involving Tony McAndrew plus a cash readjustment of £60,000 for the player. The board in their infinite wisdom accepted the deal.

Now you're not trying to tell me Darren Wood was valued at only £60,000 more than McAndrew, even acknowledging the 100 per cent player that Tony was, remembering the keen interest from Anfield only 18 months previously. Chelsea and particularly John Neal must have been amazed to sign a player of such potential so cheaply.

The Darren Wood transfer highlights, only too vividly, the eccentricities of a board which was having to sell its playing assets in order to meet the club's debilitating weekly running costs.

There is no doubt whatsoever in my mind that the crucial turning points in Middlesbrough's modern day fortunes, which led to the club's ignominious relegation from the First Division, can be directly traced back to firstly, the FA Cup quarter final defeat at the hands of an unfancied Wolverhampton Wanderers side in March 1981 and, secondly, the breaking of the club's accepted wage structure in an effort to retain the services of one particular player.

There was understandable bitter disappointment among both the players and the long-suffering supporters when history repeated itself and Boro once again failed to reach an FA Cup semi-final. The end of the Wembley dream was more than some fans could stand and led to a very noticeable and rapid decline in local morale towards the football club.

People often accuse directors of being impassive and not caring about the team but I felt just as downhearted and shattered as the supporters on that black night at Molineux.

It was after that defeat I decided John Neal was not up to the manager's job. He lacked the drive and motivational skills needed to maintain the respect of the dressing room and as a result there was a developing crisis of confidence within the club. It was therefore unanimously felt by the board that the only possible course of action was to dispense with his services and give him a cash settlement.

The fans' anger at the time was further fuelled when Craig Johnston unwisely stated in public his desire to leave Ayresome Park for Anfield at the end of 1980/81 season. He told the directors:

"I want treating like a million pound player."

That was a daft and immature remark to make. He hadn't even played two full seasons in the first team. His self-centred attitude also led to some rather unsavoury scenes at the remaining home games with his car being vandalised. That reaction, which was borne out of sheer supporter frustration, only hastened Johnston's departure to Liverpool. Quite frankly I was glad to be rid of him and his playboy image because I felt he had no long-term commitment to the Boro. It was also scant reward for the club which had given him his opportunity in professional football.

The turbulent summer of 1981 was punctuated by a series of shock and unexpected departures from Ayresome Park.

The long serving and ever reliable David Armstrong personally requested an immediate transfer and when he explained to me the depth of his complicated personal problems I had no choice but to grant him his request. I would never have accepted a transfer request from David in any other circumstances and I certainly did not want him to leave.

I even proposed at a board meeting that he should be given a token of our appreciation for the loyal service he had given the club but it was vetoed by certain directors, which I thought was rather hardhearted. He was quickly bought by Lawrie McMenemey of Southampton for their record transfer fee of £600,000, but considering the amount of games he eventually played for them it was money well spent.

Quickly following on from Armstrong's enforced departure, out of contract Mark Proctor was vigorously pursued by Brian Clough of Nottingham Forest. Proctor was transferred for £440,000, although it must be said he never really fulfiled his earlier potential once he left Middlesbrough. Other established players like the popular Bosco Jankovic also left during the close season, so the heart was effectively ripped out of what had been, only a few months earlier, a promising young team.

The board, during that period, were heavily criticised by the supporters for not trying hard enough to keep their best players. The criticism was wholly unjustified and without foundation. Harold Shepherdson, George Kitching and myself spent many hours in discussions with various players, trying to negotiate new contracts, but the plain fact of the matter was that Middlesbrough Football Club was in no position to compete with the larger clubs in regard to incentives, bonuses, long term contracts and the possibility of winning trophies and medals.

We lost our stars because of the contractual changes that came into being in 1979 which allowed the players greater freedom of movement. Another important contributory factor was the creeping involvement of agents who demanded perks for their clients in terms of tax free signing on fees and cars, on top of the negotiated basic salary and bonus schemes. That private and confidential information was never released (and still isn't) into the public domain. In other words the fans are never fully aware of the wheeling and dealing that goes on behind the scenes before a player signs for a club. The final transfer fee, often quoted in the press, is just the tip of the iceberg in terms of a club's contractual commitment to a player.

In the contemporary game there seems to be little obligation or professional morality on behalf of some players to even fulfil the terms of their contracts, which appear to be totally worthless as legal documents.

Prior to the freedom of contract changes, which blew a hole in the club's wage structure, Middlesbrough FC had a sound salary system which rewarded status, seniority and loyalty to the club. We must have been doing something right when players of the calibre of John Hickton, Stuart Boam, John Craggs, Jim Platt, David Mills and David Armstrong all stayed at the club for many seasons.

I went on the record in 1979 with regard to the contract changes and stated in the press: *"That this will be the death of football as we know it,"* and I have seen nothing in the events which have unfolded since then, to make me change my mind.

The result has been that the more powerful clubs with the greater financial clout are able to trawl the market for the best players and dictate the size of transfer fees. That effectively prices other clubs out of the market place.

As we are seeing today in the Premier League, football is creating a small group of elite clubs backed by the capital investment of individual entrepreneurs or a Stock Market flotation.

In the contemporary game, if a club cannot command crowds of 30,000 plus and generate a large revenue from commercial enterprise, then they will simply be making up the numbers.

It is my belief that in the future, the Premier League will only ever be won by an elite number of teams and Middlesbrough may never be one of them. It would, however, give me the greatest of pleasure to be proved wrong, but I find myself concerned about the future of Middlesbrough FC, new stadium and all. I doubt whether there is the depth of support on Teesside to sustain the club financially in the long term. But I do admire the current regime's drive and determination to succeed.

The eventual in-house appointment of Bobby Murdoch in June 1981 was seen by the board as a safe pair of hands. Since finishing as a player he had been on the Ayresome Park coaching staff and knew most of the players well. Therefore it was felt he would be starting the job from a position of strength. In the summer of 1981, contrary to popular opinion, the club had no outstanding debts and was in a healthy financial state to start the new season.

Unfortunately the players bought by Murdoch, such as Mick Baxter and Joe Bolton, were later proved to be inadequate and the team struggled from day one when they were beaten at home by Tottenham's Argentine imports.

I have often been asked what happened to the "big" money from the transfer sales of 1981. The simple answer is that all the revenue was used to buy new players and cover the cost of the rising wages and signing on fees demanded by players. Not one penny of the transfer money was ever diverted to fund other projects such as the Sports Hall. That was funded wholly from other sources, which will be fully explained later.

David Hodgson was a prime example of where some of the money went. At the start of the 81/82 season he was only 20 years old and had one year of his current contract to run. Bobby Murdoch wanted him to sign an extension to that contract but his personal demands were so high that I insisted he brought his father into the club to negotiate on his behalf.

At that time, most of Middlesbrough's top players were on a good basic weekly wage. Hodgson wanted nearly double the basic, plus bonuses, a tax free lump sum and a new car every two years. I was so dismayed by his avaricious attitude that I left the meeting and referred the matter to the board of directors. Bobby Murdoch desperately wanted Hodgson to re-sign in an effort to raise flagging public morale. After the loss of so many star players one of the directors suggested we would be "hung drawn and quartered" if we didn't keep Hodgson at the club. So the decision of the board, which I voted against, was to accede to his demands.

Hodgson and his father were asked, and promised, to keep the new deal to themselves in case the contents of his contract led to dressing room unrest, particularly among the more experienced players. Remember, at that time, great servants such as John Craggs and Jim Platt were still at the club and were earning nowhere near the money being offered to Hodgson to entice him to stay.

There was a very public re-signing session done in the full glare of local publicity. The average supporter, however, was totally oblivious to the money it was costing Middlesbrough to keep Hodgson and with attendances declining, it was another drain on the club's financial resources.

Further problems did ensue later, however, when Hodgson declared the contents of his contract in a broadcast interview and it doesn't take a genius to realise the subsequent effect that revelation had on the team's morale. It only served to hasten the club's relegation from the First Division.

Photo call for the players and officials of Middlesbrough in 1975. Stuart Boam and I chat in the middle of the front row.

CHAPTER TEN

Resignation

The appointment of the easy going and softly spoken Scot, Bobby Murdoch, as manager of Middlesbrough in the summer of 1981 was, with the benefit of hindsight, an error of judgement. But I was not prepared for the volume of verbal vitriol and level of physical violence directed towards my family as a consequence of the team's poor start to the season.

Like Jack Charlton and John Neal before him, Bobby Murdoch was always given the board's fullest support. In fact it was an established, if unwritten, club policy that the directors did not interfere in any of the manager's transfer dealings. We were totally prepared to back Murdoch's professional expertise because, after all, he'd played football at the very highest international level and should have been able to assess the ability and potential of the players he wished to sign.

It quickly became apparent, however, even after the first few games of the new season when we found ourselves at the foot of the First Division table, that Murdoch's team was going to struggle to stay in the top flight.

As the club's poor performances continued throughout the autumn of 1981, so the supporters' anger and frustration towards me as chairman of the board intensified, beginning with the constant monotonous, derogatory and abusive chanting which escalated into deliberate physical jostling by the crowd at most of the home games. I was deeply suspicious that the demonstrations of dissatisfaction on the terraces were being well orchestrated and carefully organised by certain influential individuals whose future long term agenda for the club did not include me.

I also think those turbulent events need to be put into some sort perspective and context of importance. Remember, we are talking here about a game where, for 90 minutes each week, 22 young men wearing coloured shirts and shorts, kick a bladder of wind around a green field marked out with whitewash in order to entertain people. It has nothing at all to do with life or death, contrary to the sentiments expressed, wrongly in my opinion, by the legendary manager of Liverpool, Bill Shankly. But the behaviour of a minority of so called Middlesbrough supporters during those few months can only be described as despicable and callous in the extreme.

As the chairman of the football club I accepted, and stated publicly, that it was my overall responsibility to address the problems as they materialised and, believe me, I tried my utmost to do so. However the persistent level of violence both verbal and physical directed towards the Amer family during that period was totally unwarranted.

At its height, the embitterment towards us became so intense that youths would congregate outside the entrance to my house and hurl abuse at my wife, even going so far as banging on the windows and kicking the side of her car as she drove by.

I found those contemptible actions particularly abhorrent, as Margaret's only connection with the football club was that she happened to be married to Charles Amer, and targeting her as a means of applying pressure on me, was shameful and unforgivable.

The creeping campaign of intimidation continued one particular evening when the obscene graffiti was daubed along my driveway in gloss paint. It cost me hundreds of pounds to have the unrepeatable remarks and suggestions removed from the tarmac.

The wooden fencing at the entrance to Normanby Hall was also constantly vandalised and eventually four of the culprits were taken to court and fined £200 each, placed on probation, and ordered to pay £400 in compensation towards the damage they'd caused. It appeared to me a new game called "Taunt the Amers" was rapidly becoming the fashionable local pastime.

Often, as I went out of the house, I was jeered by the afore-mentioned youths and in fact the harassment became so acute that the police themselves even suggested they should provide me with personal protection.

I repeat again that the menacing state of affairs arose as a direct result of the town's football team experiencing their first really poor season since the club had been relegated to the Third Division in 1966. Surely those mediocre performances didn't warrant the unlawful behaviour that became a regular ongoing occurrence. In fact under my chairmanship we had spent the longest continuous period in the top flight since World War Two and that is an achievement of which I am justly proud, and one that has still not been eclipsed today.

As the demonstrations of supporter discontent intensified, coffins were even paraded through the streets of Middlesbrough town centre by sombre faced pall-bearers to symbolically signify the death of the club. The whole situation quickly descended into a black melodrama and of course my own personal predicament proved to be good headline copy for both the local and national press.

The incessant persecution and long running catalogue of victimisation which affected the normal day to day life of my family, and also had a significant detrimental effect on the trade and reputation of our hotel business, culminated in a particularly nasty, cold, calculated and vicious incident when I was deliberately ambushed and stoned at the entrance to Normanby Hall.

Damaged fencing at the entrance to Normanby Hall was only a small part of the constant campaign of vandalism endured by the Amer family in 1981/82.

The ambush on me was premeditated, well organised and carefully planned to inflict injury. It occurred early one evening after the team had lost another match at Ayresome Park. I returned home to find a large branch lying across the driveway, blocking the entrance to Normanby Hall. As I got out of the car to remove it, I naively thought the wind must have caused it to fall. As I began lifting the obstruction, suddenly and without warning, I became the target for a prolonged barrage of stones and missiles which rained down on me from every conceivable direction, painfully striking all parts of my body and eventually rendering me semi-conscious and disorientated.

As the cowardly perpetrators ran away I somehow managed to stagger back into the relative safety of my car, where I sat in a state of numbed disbelief and shock at what had happened to me in the grounds of my own home. It was a vicious and unprovoked assault which resulted in me sustaining very severe and extensive bruising, particularly to the arm which had been badly injured in my motorbike accident.

In fact since the attack I have noticed a steady deterioration in the arm's mobility to such an extent that I now have very little feeling in my right thumb. The aftermath of that appalling incident made me finally question the point of me remaining as chairman at Ayresome Park if all it was going to achieve was to place the well-being of the Amer family in serious jeopardy.

As a family, we were very angry and felt there was no justification for the revengeful treatment we received. It appeared at the time that events were escalating out of control and gradually developing into something much more sinister than just the normal acceptable displays of football supporter discontent when the local team is underachieving. That type of criticism goes with the territory.

After detailed discussions regarding my position, particularly with my son Kevan, I concluded, that despite my longstanding affection for the club, there was nothing more important than the safety of my family and the security of our business future. So, on the basis of those criteria alone, I tended my resignation as chairman of Middlesbrough FC on February 14, 1982.

After some persuasion, I remained on the board in an advisory capacity only, until a suitable replacement could be found, with George Kitching taking over as chairman and the ambitious Michael McCullagh elected as his deputy.

Resigning firstly as chairman and eventually from the board of Middlesbrough FC ended a 20 year association with, and total commitment to, improving the status of my home town club.

Examining the severe bruising sustained to my right arm after I was deliberately stoned in the grounds of my own home.

During my years on the board I saw the club prosper in the 1970s under my chairmanship and restore a sense of pride to its success starved supporters. I worked tirelessly, and for no personal gain, to update the antiquated facilities at Ayresome Park, and for many years I personally carried and fully guaranteed any bank overdraft to ensure that the club always had transfer money available for our managers.

No other directors, with the notable exception of Jack Hatfield Jnr, displayed any willingness to help the club financially and that was the nub of the problem. The club needed a massive cash injection to move it forward but Ernest Varley captured the mood of the majority of the directors by stating at one particular board meeting: "Only a fool would invest money in a football club."

Once I had officially announced, of my own free will, my decision to step down as chairman the public reaction I received was in stark contrast to the perpetual acrimony which had gone on before. Ironically even the coffin carriers came in person to see me saying they hadn't wanted me to resign, only to do something to rectify the club's perilous position.

I also received many letters of support from fans expressing their regret at my decision to resign and acknowledging what had been achieved at Middlesbrough Football Club under my chairmanship. I particularly appreciated the tributes from the local council. For example the former leader of Middlesbrough Council, Charles Shopland, stated in a press interview in February 1982:

" In the 27 years I have known Mr Amer I have always found him to be one of the most generous men in the town of Middlesbrough. It was disturbing to see a very small minority of the football public interfering in the lives' of his family. He has given exceedingly good service to Middlesbrough FC and I would hate him to go out on a sour note because there is a large section of the Teesside public who share my view that Mr Amer has done a great deal to promote the area."

After all the trauma of the previous months it was satisfying to know that my two decades with the football club had not gone totally unnoticed in some quarters. But that belated reaction could never fully compensate for the distress both my family and I had suffered, all in the name of football.

Although the thugs achieved their objective and removed me from office I still feel even now there can be no justification whatsoever for the orchestrated personal witch-hunt I endured during those bleak days of 1981/82. I didn't want to stand down as chairman because by nature I am not a quitter. My usual reaction in times of adversity is to confront any problems which arise head-on, until they are finally resolved. I would have relished the opportunity to rectify the club's predicament but football supporters only live for today and want instant solutions to contemporary problems and that is a situation which is not unique to Middlesbrough FC. But the overriding deep concern I had for the welfare of my family and the future of our business commitments made the final decision to stand down relatively easy.

To this day I am certain that if I had remained as chairman, Middlesbrough Football Club would never have gone into liquidation in 1986. Granted, we may well have been relegated from the First Division because I fully accept we were a very mediocre team at that time, but the club's financial position would have remained stable.

What the restless fans and even certain directors failed to realise or understand was that once I had resigned, the club's bank overdraft guarantee went with me, and there was nobody else on the board who would make such a financial commitment to the club.

The rapid changes of chairmanship after my resignation and the lack of an accreditable sole guarantor also caused great unease at the bank and without doubt those circumstances were partly instrumental in launching the club on the downward spiral towards liquidation.

In an indirect way it was also the violent actions of those impatient supporters who were determined to force my resignation which set in motion a chain of events that saw the club plummet quickly into debt and to eventually teeter on the edge of footballing extinction.

At the same time as I was collaborating with this book, a similar situation developed at Manchester City where supporter protests forced the resignation of chairman Peter Swales, who was replaced by the fans' choice, former player Francis Lee. Since reluctantly stepping down, poor Mr Swales has died and we can only speculate as to the contributory factors leading to his premature death. Ironically City are now in an even worse position having been relegated from the Premier League with ever mounting debts and a succession of failed managers.

The moral of the story is that short term change brought about by "fan power" does not necessarily guarantee a football club any long term benefit.

CHAPTER ELEVEN

The So Called Great White Elephant

The content of this chapter should provide the reader with a more precise and balanced understanding of the events and circumstances which surrounded the redevelopment of the Ayresome Park football ground between 1973 and 1982. It will concentrate wholly on the facts and specifically address the insubstantial material contained in a recent publication which believes me to be dishonourable, an accusation that I find both deeply offensive and totally without foundation.

I also wish to emphasise that these recollections can be underpinned with all the relevant detailed legal documentation which formed the basis of my successful High Court libel action against the Private Eye magazine and I can give my unequivocal guarantee that this account of the events is as accurate as the passage of time will permit.

For the purposes of information, the board of Middlesbrough Football Club during the period in question included Charles Amer (chairman), George Kitching, Ernest Varley, Keith Varley, Kevan Amer, Dr.Neil Phillips (who resigned for personal reasons), Michael McCullagh and Jack Hatfield Jnr.

The building of the Sports Hall at Ayresome Park has been cited as the main cause of the original club's liquidation in the summer of 1986. That assertion, I have to say, was pure fantasy and primarily the invention of an ambitious, keen, but ultimately naive chairman who was fortunate that the shoulder of blame for Middlesbrough's dire financial position in the months following my resignation was conveniently switched on to an opportune scapegoat, who was Charles Amer.

For the first time in the public domain these are the facts about my involvement with the development of the Sports Hall at Ayresome Park.

In the 1970s the directors of Middlesbrough Football Club unanimously agreed to update the spartan facilities of their windswept Hutton Road training ground which it was felt were not comparable with the club's First Division status. As chairman, my overall objective was to help Middlesbrough Football Club to compete on an equal footing with the likes of Liverpool, Leeds United and Manchester United and if that goal was to be achieved then the club needed to dramatically improve the standard and quality of its amenities at that time.

Preliminary discussions with regard to the availability of supplementary funding were held with the Sports Council and the Labour Government's Sports Minister Dennis Howell, who I must say has probably been the most able man to hold that position since World War Two. The outcome of that consultation process was twofold. Firstly it was established that the club would be able to take full advantage of the generous grants available through the Sports Council, the Ground Development Trust and the Safety of Sports Grounds Trust, and secondly, it was decided that all our resources should be concentrated not at Hutton Road, but on a centrally located purpose built community facility attached to Ayresome Park above the existing car park at the Warwick Street side of the ground.

At this juncture it is very important to emphasise that the proposed development was a government backed initiative and not, as was implied in some misinformed quarters, an unplanned half-baked scheme cooked up by the board at that time. All the directors of Middlesbrough FC acted in good faith, based on the sound advice received on behalf of a respected Labour Minister and his department.

A crucial distinction also needs to be drawn when using certain terminology about that specific construction.

The Sports Hall was precisely that, a large hall with dressing room accommodation with proposed additional facilities including spectator seating, a gymnasium, squash courts, coffee bar and toilets. Those amenities formed only part of the ongoing phased redevelopment of Ayresome Park which began in the early 1970s.

That redevelopment, called the complex, continued throughout my chairmanship and included from 1974, the building of a souvenir shop, new boiler house, lottery office, police room, new electricity sub-station and the purchase of land at the junction of Ayresome Street and Ayresome Park Road to provide extra parking for over 50 cars. A fully licensed restaurant with bar and function suites, was also built above the club shop to service any future executive boxes and the board also hoped, by opening them to the public at lunchtime, they would become a popular venue with local businessmen.

All the above facilities were paid for by 1978 and it must be strongly emphasised that at no time did they become an issue of controversy as they were fully utilised by many appreciative patrons, including the club's directors.

The redevelopments were built with full planning approval and were funded by using a combination of the agency grants available and the profits from the club's own lottery, which by law could only be used for ground improvements which benefited the comfort and safety of the supporters.

It was also importantly agreed that the primary use of the Sports Hall's facilities would be jointly shared between Middlesbrough FC and the youth of the local community.

The grants that were available in the late 1970s from the Sports Council and Football Ground Improvement Trust certainly made the proposed development an attractive financial proposition and when complete, it would have given Middlesbrough FC a prestigious indoor training facility comparable with any club in the country at that particular time.

It is worth highlighting at this point that at no time during the initial discussion stages of the project were there any official objections from the other directors. In fact to a man, after considering the advice given on behalf of the Sports Minister, they were all enthusiastically behind the new Sports Hall development and the collective decision to proceed with the scheme was taken and minuted at a meeting of the full board on December 20, 1978.

Much needed renovation work, for which I was officially thanked by the board for saving the club thousands of pounds, had already commenced in earnest on the ageing ground when in 1976 Parkway Estates complied with the stringent legal requirements of the Safety of Sports Grounds Act and replaced the old wooden fencing that ran along the alleyway behind Ayresome Park's North Stand with a substantial brick wall. In addition, solid concrete base supports were laid on which any future construction work could be erected.

Those grant funded structures had passed a rigorous building inspection and were fully paid for prior to the commencement of any work on the new development. The land itself had been previously purchased from Shaw's Workingmen's Club around 1969 and was being utilised as a car park by the club's officials and directors.

Working from my basic designs, Ken Tytler drew up the formal plans for the Sports Hall and George Gowland, a highly respected design engineering expert, who had done work for prestigious construction projects all over the world, undertook the calculations.

The completed plans were prominently displayed in Harry Green's office for all to see. They aroused a great deal of local interest and Ernest Varley was particularly keen for observers to view the drawings. He would often be seen giving impromptu seminars about the proposed development. His initial enthusiastic endorsement was however in complete contrast to the attitude he adopted later when, for some unknown reason, he became totally opposed to the opening of the Sports Hall.

When the draft plans were made public, numerous members of Middlesbrough Council personally conveyed their delight to me that the facilities were also to be used by the local community. The terraced housing surrounding Ayresome Park was totally lacking in any worthwhile social amenities and we received nothing but praise and positive encouragement from local government officials to continue with the development.

The whole project was constructed adhering strictly to the 1976 Building Regulations and on February 2, 1979 the Borough Council gave planning permission, subject to the usual conditions, for the building work to commence. That was followed later by formal planning permission for the gymnasium and squash courts.

On the rare occasion when our adherence to the established procedures was publicly questioned we received a full and formal apology from a prominent Middlesbrough Town Councillor, withdrawing his comments and innuendo.

Contrary to further uninformed opinion, written and verbal telephone tenders were received for the work from steel erectors and plumbing, heating and roofing contractors. That tendering procedure, undertaken with the full consent of the Sports Council, was an essential prerequisite of all grant applications and no agency funding would have been forthcoming if the club had not complied with the stipulated legal requirements. What a shame those individuals who made false accusations claiming I neglected the whole tendering process didn't check their facts more thoroughly before making public statements which they later had to retract.

Before and after. Part of the ongoing major renovations of Ayresome Park undertaken during my chairmanship in order to comply with safety legislation.

As work progressed, twice weekly visits by experienced council building inspectors ensured that all aspects of the construction process were being closely monitored. Any advice given by those experts was always fully implemented. I also regularly visited the site to personally oversee the general progress and an experienced building manager from Parkway Estates was always in attendance to supervise the work.

I had the fullest cooperation at all times of the then chairman of the Council and planning officials. Any minor difficulties which did arise, and there were some on a project of that size and nature, were addressed amiably by liaising fully with the appropriate departments and following the correct procedures.

The Fire Service's Chief Safety Officer drew up the plans, based on my drawings, for the safety lighting, alarm system and extinguisher positions and on July 14, 1980 the County Fire Officer confirmed in writing that he had no objection to the Sports Hall being used to stage boxing matches or dances with maximum attendances of around 1,000 people.

In November 1980, after a full inspection, it was also interesting to note when initial licensing applications were made in Teesside Magistrates Court that the members of the bench, after visiting the site for themselves, were very complimentary about the proposed development and that positive sentiment was typical of the local reaction we were receiving with regard to the facilities.

Also, throughout the licensing process, comprehensive advice was given by Cleveland Police Licensing Officers and indeed they also were very complimentary in court on February 4, 1981, when they affirmed that all licensing procedures for the development had been completed to their absolute satisfaction.

Another popular misconception which needs to be corrected, particularly for the club's supporters, was the constant accusation that money was being diverted from the transfer dealings of that time to pay for the Sports Hall. It just wasn't true.

In fact the transfer dealings of John Neal and Bobby Murdoch, coupled with the falling gate receipts and the spiralling cost of players' wages, resulting from the freedom of contract, ironically meant there was no surplus money available to be directed towards the construction. It simply didn't exist.

For example, when Graeme Souness was sold to Liverpool and we later bought Irving Nattrass from Newcastle, the deficit on those deals alone was over £150,000.

The financial reality was that transfer fees in the late 1970s and early 1980s were escalating out of all proportion and despite keeping our admission prices to a minimum, as well as providing 400 free match day tickets for the children of the unemployed families, the money generated through the Ayresome Park turnstiles was not enough to cover our overheads.

Any transfer income received by the club, therefore, had to be used as legitimate cash flow to pay the everyday bills, such as players' salaries. And with most of the directors unwilling to inject any personal capital into the club, like all businesses we had to budget accordingly.

The new development had to be, and most certainly was, wholly self-financing using the grants received from the Sports Council, the Football Grounds Development Trust, the League's Safety of Sports Grounds Trust, a loan from Scottish and Newcastle Breweries, Parkway Estates and by utilising the profits from the club's own lottery fund which could only be invested in new projects such as the Sports Hall.

All of the money from these sources amounted to more than £1m and not one penny of it came from anywhere else. These are the facts and no amount of innuendo, half-truths or misinformation can alter them.

To further underpin the point I am making, according to the club figures from 1977-82, the amount of revenue generated by the sales of players during that period was £3.22m. The total expenditure, over the same period, spent on new players, accommodation, cars, re-signing bonuses, increased wage costs and subsidising working losses caused by falling gate receipts was £3.58m.

The overall deficit, in excess of £300,000, only serves to reaffirm my contention that there was no spare capital available to be redirected to the Sports Hall development. The finance had to be generated from other bona fide sources.

It must also be emphasised in the strongest possible terms that in July, 1981, other than the normal month to month trading accounts, Middlesbrough had no outstanding debts and no bank overdraft. Secretary Harry Green was meticulous with regard to the punctual payment of all the invoices and the club had few financial worries at that time.

During my chairmanship a great deal of money was invested on upgrading Ayresome Park for the mutual benefit of the players and supporters and I can account for every penny of that expenditure. In fact, over the years the amount of unpaid time that I devoted to Middlesbrough Football Club was often to the detriment of my family and our own business interests.

I most certainly have nothing to reproach myself for, because all of my decisions were taken in the best interests of the club and, with the passage of time, I have not changed my viewpoint.

I reiterate that no transfer money was specifically diverted to redevelop the ground or build the Sports Hall at the expense of strengthening the team.

In order to qualify for the Sports Council's grant deadline, at the end of March 1979, the whole board fully approved the choice of Parkway Estates to develop the new facility.

There was nothing unusual about the choice of Parkway to upgrade Ayresome Park as it had become a regular and established method of operation since I'd undertaken, at short notice, the highly praised and cost effective renovations of the ground for the 1966 World Cup.

Again it must be noted that at no time were there any dissenting voices on the board about Parkway's involvement in the project. If there had been any indication of disapproval I would have withdrawn our services immediately. In truth the majority of the directors were quite happy to stand back and allow Parkway to undertake the construction, as long as they could eventually take the plaudits and bask in the kudos of the completed development.

During the whole of the construction process I insisted on regular board meetings to update and inform the directors of the latest developments in the building programme. One director in particular, when confronted with the relevant technical information often retorted: "You're the expert, you know what you're doing, carry on with it."

I took that type of endorsement to mean I had the directors' complete trust and backing at all times.

Unfortunately political events beyond our control took a hand in the amount of finance that was readily available for the project.

When the Conservatives won the General Election of October 1979 and Margaret Thatcher became Prime Minister, one of her first directives was to freeze all building grants. As a result of that totally unexpected ruling, we found ourselves in the position of having to share our grant with Carlisle United, on the understanding that in the long term the final amount of funding we received would be unaffected. To ensure the building work could continue without any major interruptions, that grant shortfall was carried solely by my company, Parkway Estates.

As the construction progressed, all of Parkway's work was carefully itemised on the relevant invoices which were then given to the club's secretary Harry Green. The payment cheques were signed on behalf of the club by authorised personnel and all the invoices for the Sports Hall were formally included in both Parkway Estates' and Middlesbrough FC's accounts.

Those accounts were then audited at least twice a year by Middlesbrough Football Club's official accountants, who found nothing untoward in any of the financial transactions carried out between the two parties. Those findings, I feel, speak volumes for the legitimacy of the collaboration and pours cold water on the claims that I somehow abused my position at the football club's expense.

It must also be highlighted that on numerous occasions, particularly when I was preparing for litigation and voluntarily cooperating with relevant authorities after Middlesbrough Football Club was liquidated in 1986, my financial involvement with the club was carefully scrutinised in the minutest detail by the Inland Revenue, VAT inspectors, Safety of Sports Ground accountants, Ground Improvement Trust finance advisors, Sports Council advisors and the Official Receiver's assistant. The findings of all those professional agencies concluded that there was no misappropriation of the club's funds. In some cases recommendations were even made that I was, in fact, grossly undercharging the club for the amount of work I'd undertaken on their behalf and all the directors knew it.

Following each rigorous audit, every director would be given a profit and loss balance sheet which outlined the club's expenditure under specific headings. During those meetings I was always available to answer any queries or questions raised by the directors with regard to the finance being invested in the development. But at no time was there any discernable dissatisfaction with the detailed information they received. I therefore deduced from that positive reaction that the board was more than content with the progress being made.

When the Sports Hall was nearing completion, the formal title of "The Ayresome Sporting Club" was suggested as a name to cover all the new facilities, including the already opened bar and restaurant.

The directors held meetings to prepare a grand opening ceremony. Details about promotional brochures, Ayresome Sporting Club logos, equipment and staffing were all well advanced and a guest list of local dignitaries, heads of sporting organisations and school representatives compiled.

Former Boro favourite Frank Spraggon was appointed Sports Hall manager.

During 1981, prior to any formal opening ceremony, around 150,000 people utilised the facilities free of charge and many wrote complimentary letters to the club's commercial manager, Duncan Gibson, and Frank Spraggon. Enquiries and applications about hiring the sports facilities, on a more permanent basis in the future, were received from over 100 groups including Teesside Polytechnic, Barclays Bank, Cleveland Youth Association and Cleveland Social Services, which only further served to emphasise the local community's positive belief in the hall and its undoubted potential.

That overwhelming level of endorsement was surely proof enough of both the quality and standard of the amenities. Even the sports administrators who helped to finance the project had no doubts about its excellence as Bill Saunders, the northern regional director of the Sports Council said: "On my last visit, I saw an absolutely superb place and when we looked at the costings we didn't know how it could have been produced at the price."

May 1981 and the pristine Sports Hall looks anything but a white elephant as I view the spotless facility with left to right, George Kitching, Bill Sinclair, editor of the Evening Gazette and Harry Green.

Other leading football clubs made formal enquires about the development and one in particular, Nottingham Forest, were very keen to build a facility of a similar nature at their City Ground.

Visiting directors who came to Ayresome Park for matches during seasons 80/81 and 81/82 were shown around the Sports Hall. They all made complimentary comments about what they saw and some even told me how envious they were of the development.

Combining all the above comments together certainly provides a strong body of evidence in favour of the Sports Hall and proves that the standard of the facilities in no way deserved the concentrated and derogatory criticism they later received after my resignation, when convenient scapegoats were being sought on which to apportion blame for the club's financial problems.

The burning question which needs answering is: How did a development which had the total backing of the board, both at its inception and during its construction, suddenly become such a perceived millstone around the neck of the club, despite the obvious depth of support for the facility within the local community and beyond?

The answer to that conundrum lies buried deep within the internal politics and personal conflicts which manifested themselves between individual board members at that time.

As with most organisations there are those lesser minions or "nothing men" who aspire and conspire to accede to positions of power, and the board of Middlesbrough FC was no different. Personal grievances which had apparently been simmering under the surface for quite some time came to head when certain directors, who had played little or no part in the redevelopment of the ground, except to continually approve my building work, formed an aggressive reactionary faction within the board.

The seeds of the discontent were probably sown when the membership of the Sports Hall management sub-committee was discussed. During the construction period it became patently obvious that Jack Hatfield's background in the sports business and his keen interest in the project made him the prime candidate to chair the sub-committee. However, when that suggestion was proposed by Kevan Amer, one director in particular felt aggrieved at being passed over for the position. Once that decision was made an irreconcilable split developed in the boardroom.

It was followed by deliberate delaying tactics being placed in the way of the official opening from other quarters and a concerted whispering campaign about the quality of workmanship and provision of adequate safety measures also began.

The campaign of non cooperation gathered momentum during the autumn of 1981 when the team performed very badly and the viability of the new facilities was suddenly called into question. Unfounded accusations about the lack of investment in the playing staff proliferated. Those accusations were inaccurate because, prior to the start of the season, more than £750,000 was spent on buying Mick Baxter, Joe Bolton and Heine Otto. At the same time my family was subjected to verbal threats and physical violence. Both my credibility as chairman and my personal integrity became the focus of close scrutiny.

Once I'd resigned as chairman, and eventually from the board, I was in no position to defend myself and it appeared that any contentious allegations about my conduct at Ayresome Park could be grossly exaggerated and made in public. Events culminated in a malicious Private Eye magazine article which provided me with the legal opportunity to finally disprove all the accusations laid against me, at the High Court in London.

I will always fondly remember a short while after Kevan and I resigned from the board, the new chairman Michael McCullagh proudly proclaiming in the media: "I want change and I won't do the job unless I'm allowed to do it my way," and "Now just watch us go!"

Well they most certainly did. They went hurtling towards liquidation and total oblivion.

Also after our resignations we were informed that no seats would be made available for us in the directors box, which I thought was rather petty, considering the amount of unpaid time and effort I'd devoted to the club over nearly two decades....Such Power!

In early 1983, as the Sports Hall stayed closed to the general public, the supposed findings of two separate investigations into alleged financial irregularities and the quality of the workmanship were officially released to the local press by the club chairman. The ridiculous statements which accompanied their release, claiming that Kevan and I had resigned from the board because of the report's damning contents, were utter balderdash.

We had never seen the building report, and on the date in question the financial report wasn't even in existence. It was finally placed before the board some four months later. So in order for Kevan and myself to resign because of the report's conclusions, we would have needed to be extremely proficient clairvoyants.

Even when we eventually saw the building standards report, which ironically cost the cash strapped club thousands of pounds to produce, no credence could be attached to its findings as it was incomplete. The authors, through no fault of their own, had not been supplied with sufficient relevant information on which to compile an accurate account.

It has been categorically stated elsewhere in this publication, that I have always built my developments to well above the required planning regulations of the time and the Sports Hall was no exception to that rule. Those facts cannot be disputed. I even volunteered to undertake, at Parkway's expense, the small amount of finishing work required, which we had not been allowed to complete because one of the directors removed Parkway's workforce from the site. That work only included extra fire protection for the nine steel centre stanchions, fire-proofing the wood panelling in the main reception area, completing the squash courts and ensuring the hall's emergency exit door complied with the relevant safety regulations.

Enabling me to complete those recommendations would have ensured that the facility received the full approval of the council's principal building inspector and could have formally opened to the public, but antagonistic prevarication emanating from the boardroom prohibited me from doing so.

When I resigned from the board of Middlesbrough FC in January 1983, the club owed Parkway Estates in excess of £120,000 for the grant shortfall that we had carried for three years. I never received the full remuneration for the work carried out because I withdrew my legal action against the club in 1985/86 after personal discussions with the then chairman, Alf Duffield, in an effort to ease the club's perilous financial crisis.

That outstanding and unpaid debt then became a worry to my own bankers because it was obvious, with the club in such dire financial straits, that the money was never going to be repaid in the foreseeable future. So, in order to pacify the bank, I had to sell Parkway's own land bank for an amount far less than its true market value and to restructure the company. Without going into the financial details, the dispiriting outcome of the transaction was that most of my long-term hardworking employees lost their jobs as a direct consequence of the actions taken by certain individuals who were failing Middlesbrough Football Club.

I have frequently been asked why I didn't follow up my threat to sue the club for the money I was owed. The answer is two-fold. Firstly, even after all the boardroom and supporter acrimony I endured, my frustration and anger was not directed towards the football club itself - because I still cared passionately about its fortunes - but at some of the board members. Secondly, and very importantly, Middlesbrough FC is sacrosanct to its loyal and devoted supporters. Imagine the consequences to my local hotel businesses, the reputation of which my family had painstakingly built up in the town over 50 years, if I was perceived to be the prime instigator of the club's ultimate demise. There was quite frankly too much at stake, both professionally and personally, so I did not pursue or demand the debt through the courts. I waited, quite legitimately, to be paid with the rest of the just creditors when the new company, Middlesbrough Football & Athletic Club 1986 Ltd, was formed.

Eventually part of the sum owing was paid after a bond was lodged with the football authorities by the new owners and the debt had been assessed by the League's own officials, the Inland Revenue's Investigating Department and VAT inspectors. All those financial experts agreed that my claim for payment was indeed an honourable request and I see no reason why the club should have been "disappointed" to settle my account.

I find it quite ironic that one of the main accusations laid against me, alleged that I used my own company Parkway Estates to secretly syphon money out of Middlesbrough FC. The plain facts of the matter were that other directors, and their relations, enjoyed free trips around the world on club tours to far flung places like Australia and Japan, and also received thousands of pounds worth of free entertainment into the bargain. Those irrefutable facts are often conveniently overlooked by the very directors who have often criticised me.

The major implication of my resignation from the board was that the club no longer had an approved guarantor at the bank and when George Kitching also resigned as chairman a few months after me, and the keen but inexperienced Michael McCullagh was appointed, the bank quickly realised that without the underwriting of such a cast iron guarantee, they had no option but to severely restrict the club's overdraft facility.

Nine games without a win at the start of the 1982/83 season resulted in the departure of Bobby Murdoch. It also dramatically reduced the team's appeal to the supporters and created a vicious circle of reduced gate receipts, which in turn led to the club being unable to cover its overheads. The net result was that debts quickly mounted to over £1m.

Those debts, it has to be said, were not helped by the flamboyant Malcolm Allison being appointed manager at the behest of Michael McCullagh in October 1982.

Allison's prodigal, self-indulgent champagne lifestyle, seemingly condoned by the chairman, ran up large hotel bills at the club's expense. His behaviour did nothing to alleviate the Boro's ever increasing financial problems and fast disappearing reputation, which reached a new low point when a group of old age pensioners who worked behind the scenes at Ayresome Park, and whose combined weekly wages only amounted to the price of a bottle of bubbly, were relieved of their duties as a cost cutting exercise.

Even the Tory MP for Langbaurgh at the time, Richard Holt, who was demanding a Government probe into the workings of Britain's industrial tribunals, criticised the football club in the chamber of the House of Commons.

Mr Holt said the transcript of Malcolm Allison's appeal tribunal against his inevitable dismissal:

"Shows how much he managed to smoke and drink in his short time at Middlesbrough, at the expense of my constituents".

During a board meeting in March 1984, at which Michael McCullagh announced that Malcolm Allison had been relieved of his managerial duties, significant changes were made in the Ayresome Park boardroom.

Ernest Varley became president of the club, and George Kitching and Jack Hatfield were offered peripheral positions as associate directors. These newly created, but totally superfluous roles, denied them attendance to board meetings and removed the voting rights from two of Middlesbrough Football Club's most knowledgeable, highly committed and long-serving directors.

But why did the chairman feel the need to make those decisions? Only he knows the answer to that question.

The role changes, which contravened the club's Articles of Association because the number of full board members fell below the official figure required, also saw David Gaster from Camerons Brewery replace Mr. R Kitching, and Miles Middleton appointed as a financial adviser.

The alterations, however, did little to stabilise a club which was now threated with a bailiff visit and had entered into a stringent package of financial measures with the bank including, exploring the ways of increasing its share value, selling its local property assets and transferring more of its playing staff to the value of £250,000.

In June 1984, acting upon the advice of their financial adviser, whose personal interpretation of Parkway's balance sheets presented a misleading picture of the company's finances, I was served with a High Court writ by the football club which included a claim for damages against Parkway Estates and allegations that I'd failed to act in the best interests of the club by building the Sports Hall.

Apparently it was in the public interest to openly release the details to the press about a possible legal action against the former chairman without giving him prior warning of their intentions. But to my mind there was no justification whatsoever for their release. It was simply the desperate act of desperate men who were trying to raise finance from any possible source and I was vigorously prepared to defend their allegations.

By January 1985 and with all the club's assets now charged to the bank as collateral, the monetary crisis, created entirely by a board lacking cohesion and constantly plagued by frequent personnel changes, was now taking on mammoth proportions. In order to stem the rising tide of debt, another possible solution adopted by the chairman Michael McCullagh was to launch a rescue mission and invite on to the board the wealthy local businessman Alf Duffield, and for him to subsequently become chairman of a now beleaguered Middlesbrough Football Club on February 21, 1985.

Duffield's financial backing, however, provided only a temporary respite from the gathering black clouds of liquidation. It must also be emphasised, that prior to him joining the board, he later claimed that he was never fully aware of the underlying gravity of the club's financial situation.

In an effort to ease the mounting financial burden, Alf Duffield even opened a separate bank account and guaranteed a substantial loan to the club on which much needed capital could be drawn. He was, ironically, thanked by the directors for his efforts in the official minutes.

During his brief time at the helm, the likeable Mr Duffield and manager Willie Maddren did in fact, despite the tight financial restraints, invest well in players. They purchased Steve Pears, Archie Stephens, Brian Laws and Bernie Slaven, all of whom were to prove vital assets in the club's re-emergence under Bruce Rioch and Colin Todd in 1986/87.

Alf Duffield was, however, swimming against a strong financial tide and with Ayresome Park crowds eventually down to below 5,000 die-hard supporters, the economic truth of the situation was becoming starkly apparent. He eventually resigned as chairman on April 15, 1986, unable to halt the club's decline.

In 1986, during the course of the liquidation proceedings, a director of the club stated under oath that the substantial six figure sums arranged by Alf Duffield on behalf of the club were in fact generous gifts donated to Middlesbrough FC by the industrialist. That claim was wholly without foundation and a deliberate "try on" to avoid the club's honourable debt repayment obligations. It also did much to belittle the efforts of a well meaning individual who had striven hard to save a club which was floundering.

Relegation to the then Third Division for only the second time in the club's history brought about the inevitable financial collapse and the uncertain summer of 1986 when it appeared that Middlesbrough FC may well cease to exist.

One begs to ask the question, where was former chairman Michael McCullagh at that traumatic time for the club. Well he'd left Ayresome Park during 1985 and in my view he's never publicly accounted for the boardroom decisions taken under his chairmanship of Middlesbrough Football Club. Like all football chairmen, no doubt McCullagh desperately wanted the club to be successful, but in my opinion he lacked the relevant experience to make the right business decisions in dealing with the evolving financial crisis, and it proved very costly.

To blame Middlesbrough FC's eventual liquidation on the building of the Sports Hall is absolute rubbish and an inadequately contrived smokescreen erected by those who were seeking to abdicate responsibility for their own unsuccessful handling of the club's affairs in the early 1980s. If the board had fully opened the facility as planned, and not been consumed by petty internal squabbling, far from being a drain on the club's resources, the Sports Hall could have provided the directors with much needed cash flow and a worthwhile link with the local community on which to build future support.

Over the last decade, sports and training facilities have now become one of the country's fastest developing growth areas, generating millions of pounds in revenue. What a shame that the Ayresome Park Sports Hall was never given the opportunity to prove its worth, even though it was one of the first to be built at a football ground. A classic case of missing the boat.

The original club's eventual demise lies squarely on the shoulders of certain directors who were undoubtedly endeavouring to use their positions on the board to enhance their own reputations within the Teesside area and beyond. If they had been financially committed towards securing the Boro's future they would have injected their own personal capital into the club, as I did on numerous occasions. And I reiterate once again, some board members only had as little as £20 in share capital invested in the club. Now how can that be described as total commitment?

CHAPTER TWELVE

Years in Limbo

After my resignation as chairman I very rarely attended any directors or shareholder meetings and I finally thought my problems with the Middlesbrough Football Club would be confined to the history books. In fact I couldn't have been more wrong. They became appreciably worse in October 1982 when a malicious article questioning my financial association with the club appeared in the business news of the supposedly humorous satirical magazine Private Eye, under the punning headline: "Amer of Industry."

Let me state categorically that I know, beyond a shadow of a doubt, who disclosed the misinformation to that puerile adult comic and I personally challenged the cowards to repeat their allegations in public. To this day, not surprisingly, they have failed to do so because quite simply their assertions were not true. They were pure fiction, deliberately invented and concocted in order to discredit my reputation both locally and nationally.

I will allow you to draw your own conclusions from the deafening silence that has ensued since the original anonymous disclosure. I feel it does speak volumes about the personal integrity of the individuals who perpetrated the whole unsavoury affair.

The groundless, threadbare and preposterous accusations made in the Private Eye article contended that Middlesbrough FC's problems in late 1982 were directly attributable to my exhibiting a financial "deftness of touch" during the transfer of certain star players, which it was also insinuated I personally sanctioned in order to raise extra capital for the construction of the Sports Hall. Further unfounded allegations were also made that I'd flouted the law by not obtaining the relevant planning permissions and the building materials acquired by Parkway Estates for the Ayresome Park development were somehow spirited away and used to build a new property for a member of my family.

After the allegation about the compatibility of the building materials was made, the new house soon became a local tourist attraction. I have to acknowledge during those trying times that my son Kevan never lost his sense of humour. On one particular occasion while he was waiting at a set of traffic lights somebody shouted at him: "Give us our bricks back."

To which Kevan succinctly replied, "I'm having the pitch next."

In hindsight there were so many inquisitive people arriving to gawp at the property, that if he'd charged them on a pay per-view basis, he would have made a handsome profit.

It was only after we eventually invited an independent assessment of the materials - the conclusion of which refuted the ridiculous claims - that our family life returned to some sort of normality. To suggest that I endeavoured to use the chairmanship for my own financial gain is nonsensical. I simply did not need to do so, because my other business interests were thriving.

I can categorically state that my son Kevan, left, was not saying to me: "Hey dad, I've just had a great idea for a new development."

I do not intend to recount the five years of tedious legal proceedings, suffice as to say, the wildly inaccurate allegations were eventually withdrawn during a lengthy litigation process at the Old Bailey and resulted in me receiving substantial libel damages against Pressgram Ltd, the publishers of Private Eye. The outcome, I felt, totally vindicated my challenge to those spurious accusations.

A statement read out in open court by our counsel Mr Geoffrey Shaw to the judge Mr Justice Caulfield recognised the Amers' commitment to Middlesbrough FC:

"Of their devotion to the club there can be no doubt," and that *"Private Eye now accepts there was no truth in the allegations whatsoever and that counsel for the defendants is here to acknowledge this and to apologise. His clients have paid a substantial sum to the plaintiffs by way of damages and costs. In these circumstances, their reputations vindicated, the plaintiffs are prepared to let the matter rest."*

Before the action was formally withdrawn, counsel for the defendants Mr Desmond Browne said that the *"very grave and hurtful"* accusations against the Amers were *"unreservedly withdrawn"* and an *"unqualified apology"* was made. I have since found out to my cost that winning a court case does not necessarily guarantee that you fully restore your tarnished personal credibility. If enough mud is repeatedly thrown in your direction eventually some appears to stick. People, thanks to being fed a constant stream of distortion, innuendo and sensationalism by the media, only believe what they want to believe. Somehow the grudging retractions are never quite as appetising as the initial juicy allegations and although our recourse to litigation was totally successful I still feel, even today, there is an undercurrent of prejudice in the Middlesbrough area which refuses to accept the truth.

Unfortunately for me it appears the name of Charles Amer will forever be synonymous with the financial demise of Middlesbrough FC because I was a convenient and high profile scapegoat for some of the misguided individuals who replaced me.

Since the original article appeared in the Private Eye my once hectic social life has been reduced to nothing. I am a proud man and those accusations effected the health of my wife and caused me great personal embarrassment. I was ashamed to meet my friends and colleagues, many of whom had been some of the most respected and well known people in the country. I deliberately curtailed all my activities with the Variety Club and National Sporting Club, the two organisations which had given me such an immense amount of pleasure over the years, because I couldn't face the constant explanations and denials of the unfounded allegations made against me. Often the principle of no smoke without fire seemed to be adopted and I became very weary of having to repeatedly defend my reputation in public.

So for the last 15 years my self imposed monastic routine has revolved around the journey from home to the Marton Hotel and Country Club to discuss business with Kevan and Philip and to meet a small circle of trusted local friends for lunch, interspersed with the occasional holiday abroad. My once stimulating social life has been effectively ruined.

I will always believe that there was an organised clandestine smear campaign to undermine my position at Middlesbrough FC based on envy and orchestrated by certain ambitious power hungry directors. Since my resignation they've had to live with the allegations perpetrated against me. Unlike me however, the ringleaders have never had to publicly account for their actions. But at least I can console myself with the fact that my conscience is clear.

Since my successful court case I've found more time to relax at our apartment in Majorca.

As highlighted in the previous chapter, I had recourse to take further retaliatory action in January 1983 when, without warning, an unsubstantiated official club press release appeared in the local newspaper, claiming that Kevan and I had resigned from the board as a direct result of the critical findings contained in two investigations allegedly undertaken on behalf of the club's directors by independent financial and building consultants.

Those were completely outrageous accusations to make. The statement was deliberately sophistical insinuating that we had resigned on the basis of those findings, and was borne out of the directors' deep sense of frustration at continually being asked by the supporters if I was still pulling the strings behind the scenes at Ayresome Park, despite my resignation.

That episode was again further evidence of the continued campaign to taint the Amer name with controversy. What was printed in the local press was pure tosh and downright uncorroborated hearsay. It led to a top level meeting with a leading newspaper executive who endeavoured to persuade me not to sue the club with regard to the original inaccurate article. I eventually accepted the opportunity for the right to reply and vigorously rebutted the press release's misrepresentation of the facts.

I will repeat again so my position is quite clear, the only reason I stepped down as chairman and eventually resigned from the board was because of the growing amount of physical violence that was specifically directed against my family and not because of any alleged financial irregularities during my association with Middlesbrough Football Club.

I had absolutely nothing to hide. That was why I was so determined to take Private Eye to court in order to give me the opportunity to present the accurate facts. Once confronted with the truth, instead of contrived fabrication, their case collapsed.

While on the subject of the press I wish to state during my time as a director and chairman of Middlesbrough FC that I believe the club was always treated fairly by the North-eastern newspapers. The late Cliff Mitchell, the well respected sports writer at the Evening Gazette, whose wife's brother was my best man, and Ray Robertson of the Northern Echo always reported the events at Ayresome Park honestly and equitably and for their unbiased professionalism I am very grateful. It was only latterly when the unsubstantiated scurrilous remarks appertaining to the club's finances were misreported that I feel I had any cause or justification for complaint because in general I felt I had a good working relationship with the local journalists.

*Every Boro' supporters favourite adopted uncle,
the Evening Gazette's Cliff Mitchell, addresses the dinner held
at the Marton Hotel to celebrate the club's promotion in 1974.*

Over the last 15 years I've had much time to carefully reflect upon my involvement at Ayresome Park. The manner of my exit will always be a constant source of personal bitterness towards certain individuals, but that emotion cannot be permitted to cloud the pride I felt in being chairman of my local team.

I joined the board of Middlesbrough Football Club with one intention and one intention only, to help establish them as one of the major football teams in the country. And for a brief period from 1974-76 I believe I achieved my objective, when we were one of the most feared and respected teams in the land. But Jack Charlton, a man for whom I'll always have immense admiration, failed to capitalise on the window of opportunity by not investing in the two or three top quality players we needed at that time. In particular we all knew the team was short of a striker, but the right signing never quite materialised and the golden chance was frustratingly lost.

As a director and chairman for more than 20 years I watched with pride many fine players wear the famous red shirt of the Boro and I would like to single out some of my favourites who gave me a great deal of pleasure over the years.

Centre-half turned striker John Hickton, who was signed for £20,000 from Sheffield Wednesday in 1966, must have been one of Boro's bargain buys of all time. He played nearly 500 games for the club and was always totally committed to Middlesbrough for over 11 years.

Full back John Craggs, signed for £50,000 from North-eastern rivals Newcastle United in 1971, was an honest lad who eventually played over 470 games in 11 distinguished seasons at Ayresome Park. Like John Hickton, he was conscientious, loyal and never involved in any controversy. A model professional.

As chairman, I also derived great satisfaction from seeing North-eastern lads establish themselves in the first team and Willie Maddren and David Armstrong were two players I particularly admired. How Willie was never capped by England I will never know. It was undoubtedly his solid partnership with Stuart Boam that was the bedrock on which the success of Jack Charlton's team was built. How sorry I was to hear of his debilitating illness.

David Armstrong was simply one of the best left footed players in the country during the 1970s. Jack Charlton called him his "little gem". He was so consistent that he eventually broke the Middlesbrough record for consecutive appearances. What a shame he was transferred due to personal reasons because I felt sure he never really wanted to leave the area.

Jim Platt, Boro's steady, quiet and reliable custodian for over a decade was again a very conscientious professional and represented Northern Ireland on numerous occasions. He would probably have won more international caps if he hadn't played in the same era as the talented and dependable Pat Jennings.

Due to my business commitments I didn't manage to travel to a great many away games but there were three clubs in particular that I enjoyed visiting.

Ipswich Town was always a very friendly and welcoming club to visit. It reminded me in many ways of Middlesbrough. We were of a comparable size and had a similar number of supporters. The Cobbold family, who owned the local brewing company, were the main shareholders of the club and chairman Patrick Cobbold always ensured that the Portman Road hospitality was first class.

At Arsenal Football Club's Highbury Stadium you became very aware of the Gunners' famous footballing history. It was a club steeped in tradition and their chairman, Peter Hill-Wood, was a real gentleman.

Another chairman for whom I had a high regard was the late Louis Edwards of Manchester United. On one particular visit to Old Trafford we were chatting in the directors' lounge before the game and he told me he was thinking of stepping down from the board because of the accusations made in the press about his alleged creative involvement in the club's financial dealings. I could do nothing at the time except sympathise with his predicament. But little did I know it would not be long before I, too, was having my own personal integrity questioned in public.

A mythical Teesside legend recounts the tale about a gypsy's curse which was supposedly cast over Ayresome Park during its construction in 1903. That incantation was widely cited by the supporters as the reason behind the club's trophyless and occasionally troubled history at the ground. Personally I believe you create your own opportunities in life and on reflection I wouldn't have changed many of the decisions I made as chairman of Middlesbrough Football Club, only some of the malevolent directors I was saddled with.

CHAPTER THIRTEEN

Inspiration and Recognition

Apart from my very close family, whose support has been a constant source of inner strength, particularly over the last decade, I have been extremely fortunate during the course of my life to have met and maintained lasting friendships with many people of great vision, talent and expertise. This postscript is to convey my appreciation to those individuals whose influence, both direct and indirect, has helped to fashion and guide my own career in entertainment and business.

Firstly I must reiterate once again, even after all this time, the deep debt of gratitude I owe to the medical staff of the now demolished North Ormesby Hospital and in particular Mr Brittain-Jones, who nearly 70 years ago personally supervised my recovery from the serious injuries I sustained in a near fatal motorcycle accident. Without their skill, patience and dedication I do not think I'd have had the opportunity to lead such a full and rewarding life. To them all, I am eternally grateful.

Without doubt the most important influence on my entertainment career was Bill Butlin. He was the man who typified the true pioneering entrepreneurial spirit. His original holiday ideas radically changed the way people spent their leisure time in this country. But above all he possessed the vital inner belief and self determination to put those ideas into practice. His management style, which was a blend of ruthless efficiency and quiet understanding, undoubtedly shaped the way I developed my own showbusiness career. Our lasting association was based on mutual professional respect and even when I left the Butlin Organisation, we remained firm friends and regularly attended a wide variety of social and charity functions together.

Gerald Bright adopted his Latinised name of Geraldo when in the 1930s he appeared at the Savoy Hotel in London with his famous Tango Band. He was a marvellous musician and Decca recording artiste who ended all his radio broadcasts with the catchphrase: "On behalf of me and the boys, cheerio and thanks for listenin'." He appeared on the Royal Command Performance in 1933 and toured the country extensively prior to World War Two. I first met him when I booked his band for a function at the Palais de Danse in Stockton. We immediately struck up a friendship and during the war years when he was working on behalf of ENSA, I organised some band concerts for him in the northern region.

Our association flourished after the war and we frequently attended Variety Club and National Sporting Club boxing evenings in the West End together until his death in May 1974. At one point in my career he offered me a full partnership in his Metronome Music Company in London, but acceptance would have meant a great deal of personal upheaval so I had to decline the lucrative offer.

Another medical man to whom I'm deeply indebted for his technical expertise was Mr Frank d'Abreu, who successfully operated on my ulcerated stomach in 1960. After the operation we developed a friendship which lasted until his death in 1996. He was married to the Queen Mother's cousin and we regularly attended social functions in London, particularly at the Cafe Royal.

Charles Forte was a man I greatly admired. Born in Italy and brought up in Scotland, he entered commerce via the family ice cream trade. He was the proprietor of one of London's first milk bars in the 1930's and used his innate entrepreneurial skills to build a very successful catering business before diversifying into hotels. When, in 1970, the Forte organisation merged with Trusthouse, to create a massive hotel chain, he became its chief executive.

In recognition of his outstanding business achievements and charity work he was awarded a well deserved life peerage in 1986.

His success encapsulates everything I admire in an individual because, like Bill Butlin, he began with the germ of an idea and very little capital and then possessed the self-motivation to turn his noumenon into reality. We regularly dined together with the Guv'nor at the Cafe Royal in London and I found him to be a very modest and unassuming man who never lost his temper. He was similar to Bill Butlin in that respect, very courteous in his face to face dealings with people, but forthright when making decisive business decisions.

A great friend of mine, the popular band leader Geraldo.

On the same night in the late 1940's as I played at the Royal Albert Hall, Geraldo was performing at the London Palladium.

Pictured at a Variety Club dinner with Stan Taylor, left, and surgeon Frank d'Abreu.

A man for whom I had the greatest respect and admiration was Harry Douglass. Like me he was proud to have been born and raised in Grangetown, near Middlesbrough, and was married to my father's sister, Edith. He was a man who never forgot his roots and after leaving school at the age of 13 he maintained a life-long association with the steel industry, immersing himself in the task of improving the pay and conditions of its employees. He became a local branch official of the union at 25 and was a member of the national executive of the Steelmakers Union five years later. After the Second World War he was elected to the Labour Party Executive, then general secretary of the Iron and Steel Trades Confederation and was an important member of the TUC general council. A devout Christian, he steadfastly dedicated himself to improving the lives of others.

When, in the 1930s, I was undergoing the numerous operations and intensive treatment on my injured arm and spent over a year in a London hospital, he came to visit me on several occasions, which I thought was very kind, but that was typical of the man.

In recognition of his unselfish efforts, the members of his own industry bestowed on him the title of "The Steelworkers Friend". He was deservedly given a peerage for his services to the industry, taking the title Lord Douglass of Cleveland. Even after he entered the House of Lords he continued to work tirelessly for workers' rights. He died peacefully in 1978 aged 76.

Leading industrialist John Harvey-Jones, who attended numerous functions at the Marton Hotel and Country Club, was a man for whom I had a high regard. He was born in Kent and spent most of his childhood in India. He joined the Navy, specialising in submarines, and became a qualified interpreter in naval intelligence. In the 1950s he had a change of career by moving to ICI Wilton on Teesside and held many of the top managerial positions before becoming chairman of the petro-chemicals division in the early 1970s.

His sometimes abrasive and forthright management style certainly delivered results but it was occasionally not appreciated or understood by everybody he worked with. He was a dynamic, very approachable, self-made man who possessed the ability to get the job done. He was free with perceptive business advice and was also one of the few people I have ever met who could, by the nature of his personality, light up a room. He has been deservedly knighted and starred in his own successful award winning television programme called Troubleshooter, where he advised small firms on how to improve their performance by applying the same straightforward business logic which had characterised his own career in industry.

To complete this final section I would like to formally acknowledge a small select group of people within the Teesside area whose conscientious work and achievement over the years I have come to respect.

During my time at Ayresome Park we were well served by specialists from the medical profession including Laurie Dunn, Mr David Muckle and Harry Dredge. Their thorough, diligent and unsung work for the football club ensured the players received the highest possible standard of physiotherapy and orthopaedic and dental care.

David Muckle in particular has since gained FIFA recognition for his pioneering work with regard to the treatment of sporting injuries and has had clinics named after him in honour of his achievements in both Japan and the USA.

Another doctor whose dedicated work deserves highlighting is Dr. Adrian Davies BSc., M.B., F.R.C.P. Over the years he has become a personal friend and has played a major role in developing South Cleveland Hospital into a centre of excellence for cardiology.

Dr S Jenkin-Evans was the son of a bishop. We struck up an instant rapport when he stayed with us at the Coatham Hotel in the late 1940s while he was working on the design and development of an advanced medical centre for the care of ICI employees within the local area. He later went on to become chairman of the Association of Industrial Medical Officers. A passionate Welshman who loved to sing, he was primarily instrumental in founding the original format for the Teesside Eisteddfod in the 1960s and it was through his dedicated promotional work in organising the initial performances and obtaining sponsorship, that the festival eventually evolved into a popular bi-annual cultural event.

Jim Roberts was a director of Barclays Bank and I wish to acknowledge that over a period of many years he gave me sound financial business advice. He later became our meticulous, efficient and trusted company secretary.

I first met Stan Thompson at a local point to point meeting. He ran a local firm of steel stockists and later became a valued member of the Variety Club's North-eastern regional committee. He was also the man who mooted the idea of constructing a permanent exhibition centre to recognise the nautical achievements of the famous explorer and navigator Captain James Cook, in Stewart Park, Middlesbrough.

Bill Carvell was my totally dependable and trustworthy building foreman at Parkway Estates. For over 30 years his dedication was much appreciated by the company. Since his well-earned retirement he has emigrated to Australia.

A dedicated politician who deserves some formal credit for over 40 years' service in local government is Ron Hall. Ron has worked tirelessly to improve the quality of life for the people of our area and is a former mayor of both Teesside and Redcar. He was also leader of Langbaurgh Borough Council and has served with distinction as chairman of the education and planning committee and is the current national chairman of the Dunkirk Veterans Association.

George Kitching's background in football meant that he was one of the few people on the board of Middlesbrough FC whose opinion I really valued. The part he played in securing the services of such quality players as John

George Rennie played sax with the well-known Roy Fox Band.

Hickton, John Craggs, Stuart Boam and Graeme Souness, amongst others, must be acknowledged, and I am pleased to record his astute contribution.

Finally to George Rennie, who before becoming a very successful estate agent, was a saxophonist with the well known Roy Fox Band and later fronted his own orchestra at the Dreamland Ballroom in Margate. In recent years George, along with George Kitching, has been one of my regular lunch companions and I would like to thank him for his steadfast support and friendship, particularly during the time when serious unfounded aspersions were cast upon my character.

George Rennie, FSVA, and I have been friends and associates for many years.

Writing these reminiscences has been both a pleasure and a constant source of frustration.

A pleasure, because it has enabled me to take stock and assess precisely what I've achieved throughout my very varied social and business life. It has also presented me with the opportunity to explain, from my own perspective, the sometimes controversial events that have been well publicised by others without them ever being in full possession of the relevant facts and information.

A frustration, because as a result of my horrific motorbike accident I've come to realise just how little of my childhood I can actually remember. Having such a large gap in the recollections of your early life somehow leaves you feeling rather incomplete.

However, after considered reflection, I must conclude that I have certainly lived my life to the full, and despite the occasional setbacks, I am proud of my achievements in both entertainment and business.

I must also acknowledge that throughout my multifarious career the loyal support of my family and friends has never waivered, and to them all I convey my heartfelt thanks and appreciation.

Margaret and I with our two sons Kevan, left, and Philip.